The Book of
Notting Hill

A Very Special Part of London

MELVIN WILKINSON

First published in Great Britain in 2006

British Library Cataloguing-in-Publication Data.
A CIP record for this title is available from the British Library.

ISBN 1 84114 508 4
ISBN 978 1 84114 508 2

HALSGROVE

Halsgrove House
Lower Moor Way
Tiverton, Devon EX16 6SS
Tel: 01884 243242
Fax: 01884 243325
Email: sales@halsgrove.com
Website: www.halsgrove.com

Frontispiece photograph: *A crowded Ladbroke Grove during the 2003 carnival. The spire of St John the Evangelist can be seen in the distance.*

Printed and bound in Great Britain by CPI Bath.

Foreword

Why, may you ask, is the former mayor of the small Wiltshire town of Warminster writing an introduction in a book about an exciting and vibrant part of London? Well, as a former teacher in service schools I have travelled and worked in many different locations, eventually finding myself in 'Rural Wiltshire', a wonderful location, but not where I originally grew up. Nor is it where Melvin Wilkinson grew up.

It has been my pleasure to have been associated with Melvin Wilkinson for over 17 years and, knowing Mel, I wondered why he would undertake the writing of a book about Notting Hill – I should have known better. Never forget your roots! Never forget your early experiences of life. Times then were good (or so we thought!), sometimes they were hard (they certainly were!), but the most essential factor is that they were fun! Life was far simpler then. *The Eagle, Girl, Dandy* and *Beano* and black-and-white television if you where lucky! The pressures of the twenty-first century had not been imagined.

Nostalgia is considered by some as the privilege of 'old age'. However, history is not nostalgia. It should and must be recorded by those who have experienced it and still have the 'feel' and 'images' of an age that created post-war Britain.

In terms of roots, what is important is the place where you grow up. It was and still is a community and should not and must not be forgotten. It is part of our national heritage. Mel has undertaken a task to ensure that his roots and memories, and those of others, are recorded. This is a wonderful idea. Personal recollections and observations. I envy his commitment.

It gives me great personal pleasure to fully endorse this work and commend the efforts of this dedicated author and researcher, my friend and fellow 'exile', Melvin Wilkinson.

Cllr Martin Baker
Mayor of Warminster 2004–2005

Acknowledgements

I would like to thank a number of people that have been invaluable in the writing of this book.

To all those that have contributed, those being Albert Peppiat, Tony Allen, Tony and Jackie Rawlings, Eddie Adams, Ninon Asuni, Bess Gordon, Victor Fergus, Maureen Marshall, Jennifer Williams, John Kinman, Gill Brett and Ray Berkem.

For those that have given permission for the use of photos and graphics. Andy Sparrow of Bloodrunners for his map of Portobello Road; Tony Sleep for his amazing photos from Frestonia; www.montessori.edu for the picture of Dr Montessori; Eamon Kentell and Neil Fraser at www.busphotos.co.uk; Chris Mostyn at National Grid for the picture of the coke carts at the gasworks; Eddie Adams for his support and old pictures; fellow exile Martin Baker, my mate Dave (Blakey) Blake and Jim Webb for the train pictures and help; carnival photos by Carla Gidden aka Lady Orange and Duncan Grisby; Stephen Lally and the STD register for the Clement Talbot photos and help; school photos from Anne Wyse, Susan Keen, Dennis Wright, Delia Guiltenane.

And my very special thanks to Rod Freeman for not getting fed up with me and for being an invaluable help. Rod, without your help this book would not have been possible.

If I have forgotten anyone please accept my apologies.

Above: *It's hard work when you're a teenager, so when you are getting on a bit a cuppa helps.*

Left: *Peter Cain sells fruit and veg from his pitch near to the junction with Westbourne Park Road. The Cain name has been seen on Portobello Road for many years.*

Contents

Just a Small Note

A rather sobering thought came to me whilst compiling this book – it occurred to me that, as a person with a mind that jumps from one task to another at the least excuse (usually in search of variety), I could probably count the number of books that I have read from cover to cover since leaving full-time education on the fingers of one hand. Not something that I am particularly proud of, but nevertheless a fact. I am of a technical nature and as such followed a career in engineering. I have always preferred to dissect things and learn by experience rather than read a manual – maybe I lack a gene or secret ability that would enliven these academic tasks. It is for these reasons that no one is more astonished at this journey of discovery that I have undertaken in writing this book than I am. I am now discovering the magic and enjoyment of the written word and am becoming a habitual bookworm.

I hope that you enjoy the observations, opinions, thoughts and ramblings that I have set down within these pages.

In addition I now look at Notting Hill through a different a pair of eyes. I see so much more that was there for me to see clearly, but was hidden from me by my lack of interest and ignorance of the neighbourhood's history. I now find it hard to walk down a road without looking around at the buildings and people. The clues of years gone by are all around us to enjoy and hopefully to preserve for future generations.

For your patience in wading through these chapters, I thank you.

Melvin Wilkinson, 2006.

Introduction

Welcome to your book – I say your book because it is, as the title suggests, a community history, a personal journey for members of the community, visitors and anyone with an interest in North Kensington.

The history of the area throws up some interesting stories; some which have been almost forgotten, while others have been written into local folklore. It is an area with many diverse cultures, but with a sense of community, the like of which has gone from many other parts of London and indeed the United Kingdom. It hosts the second-largest street carnival in the world, second only to Rio. It is a carnival that has been embraced by the local community and brings in visitors from all over Europe, if not the world.

Its architecture is distinctive, with some landmarks that have an individual character that says 'Notting Hill'. Some are beautiful while others would struggle to be called anything other than ugly. However, that doesn't mean to say they are not well-loved and important architectural gems.

We have seen this part of the borough of Kensington and Chelsea on the big screen, small screen, in books and magazines; we have heard about it on the radio, in song and in poems, but there is always more.

One of the best-loved roads in the borough is Portobello Road, a road that has spawned a multi-national mega business, small family shops and street traders. It is home to antique arcades, fruit and vegetable traders, bookshops, ethnic arts and crafts and, since the 1960s, a fashion culture that is legendary.

Just walk down the streets and who knows who you may bump into. Pop stars, actors, rich, poor, black, white and people from the four corners of the world. The street entertainers enhance the atmosphere of the market – I have seen steel bands, pan-pipe players and didgeridoo soloists. In years gone by the 'Happy Wanderers' could be seen on a regular basis winding their musical way from one end of Portobello Road to the other, while a one-man band played to an enthralled audience outside one of the pubs.

And where will we eat? In Notting Hill you can eat your way around the world without going more than a few hundred yards. The bars, restaurants, food stalls and shops will bring you anything from jellied eels and seafood to exotic Asian, Afro-Caribbean or Chinese delights. In the past the typical London speciality of pie and mash with liquor was available from two shops, one next to the railway bridge in Portobello Road and one in Golborne Road.

There have always been strong religious movements in the area, which is demonstrated in the churches, temples and chapels scattered around the borough. Some of these have become local landmarks, beautiful and highly visible.

I left Notting Hill many years ago, but it's still home – it's my roots and the place I always come back to. I am from Notting Hill and I love it.

Technical Bits

Geography, Topography and Stuff

Before we start on the personal and community parts of this book, we should first look at the technical details of the area – things such as where is North Kensington? How does it fit into the political map of England and what lies under it streets?

Well lets answer the first question, Where is North Kensington? London straddles the River Thames on the south-eastern corner of England, with Kensington and Chelsea being a borough on the western side of the city, to the north of the River Thames. Its highest point reaches approximately 100 feet above sea level. It has, since 1965, been joined with the neighbouring borough of Chelsea and received its title of 'Royal Borough' in 1901 after the death of Queen Victoria. This was given at the express wishes of Queen Victoria and was conferred upon the borough by King Edward VII. The title itself does not carry any special privileges or rights, but in terms of kudos, pride and honour it has immeasurable benefits, and it is a title held by only three other boroughs. The official title of the borough was therefore 'The Royal Borough of Kensington' until 1965, when it was joined with Chelsea to form the 'Royal Borough of Kensington and Chelsea'.

The democratic rule within the borough has evolved over the last 1,000 years or more, going from ownership by the lord of the manor to a democratically elected council empowered to represent the local constituents. As the authority of the manorial courts declined an intermediate method of governing civilian matters in the parishes developed. The church Vestries took an increasing role in the civilian business of the parishes, initially on a voluntary basis but later as a matter of legislation. The Vestries were so called because traditionally the local vicar would chair meetings in the church vestry with business mainly confined to church affairs and charitable bequests. From the seventeenth century these meetings took place on an annual basis, with male ratepayers being entitled to attend, to examine accounts and select officers. The Vestry clerk was the only paid post and this was a lifelong appointment. The Vestry would be empowered to administer justice and appoint a constable, called 'the beadle', to enforce its rulings. In addition a 'lock up' and stocks would usually be located outside the parish church for wrongdoers, drunks or vagrants.

The ecclesiastical Vestries reverted back to their original role in the 1855 London Government restructuring, and a new elected Vestry system was initiated. The new Vestries were elected by the ratepayers of the borough and, along with increased responsibilities, the appointment of three paid officers was required. The new positions were surveyor, medical officer of health and public analyst. These three positions were joined by a fourth, a public lighting engineer, in 1890. A further enhancement to the Vestry system was the building of a new vestry hall in 1880, which left the original hall to be converted into the Central Library. The 1880 building has since been demolished.

As the responsibilities of the Vestries grew they evolved into the typical local councils that we know in the early twenty-first century. The Vestries were finally swept away by the London Government Act of 1899, being replaced by borough councils, which in turn evolved over the decades.

The London County Council (LCC) came and went, and in going gave up many of its responsibilities to the local councils in the boroughs. Much of this was achieved by 1965 when a complete reorganisation of the London governing bodies was almost completed. This reorganisation saw the end of the LCC, which was replaced by the Greater London Council. At this time many of their responsibilities and functions were transferred to the boroughs.

By 1986 the GLC was also abolished, as was the Inner London Education Authority in 1990, transferring responsibilities to the local borough authorities. The devolution process was now complete.

The crest of the London County Council.

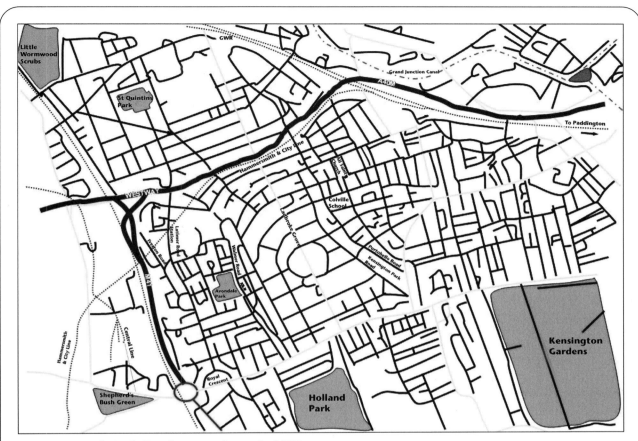

A street map of North Kensington as it was in 2005.

The coat of arms of the Royal Borough of Kensington and Chelsea.

The council of 2006 is responsible for a myriad of components that affect everyday life within a successful inner-city constituency. Amongst these are matters of education, refuse collection, leisure services and facilities, traffic and parking attendants and much, much more.

At the time of writing, the Royal Borough of Kensington and Chelsea is made up of 18 wards with a total of 54 elected councillors and employs nearly 4,500 people. The population of the borough is approximately 180,000. However, this number is swollen by some 30,000 each night by visitors staying in the borough. Its ethnic and cultural make-up is nothing short of amazing – of the 180,000 residents almost 50 per cent have origins from outside the UK. They come from some 90 different countries and speak in excess of 100 different tongues.

It has the privilege of being the smallest of the London boroughs (just over 12sq km). However, it also has the highest residential density (approx. 14,735 per sq km). It is a borough of contradictions – on one hand it is widely recognised as one of the wealthiest boroughs, and on the other it has two wards indicated in the Index of Multiple Depravation that fall into the ten per cent most deprived wards in England, those wards being Golborne and St Charles. The borough is nothing if not diverse in its make-up, and it is this that gives it its character and vibrancy, its energy and excitement.

In the Kensington and Chelsea entries in the Domesday Book we get an insight into how the area's fortunes and uses have changed over the years. For Chelsea the entry reads 'The manor covers 780 acres, containing meadows, pasture, woodland and 60 pigs.' Its value was set at £9. Kensington's entry reads 'a manor of about 240 inhabitants, a priest and three acres of vineyards, together with woodland, meadows and pasture.' Although larger than Chelsea, Kensington was only valued at £6.

The land found in this part of London is typical of the suburbs, being in the past mainly set aside for arable farming. However, it is also located on the London clay that was so important in carving out the character of Notting Dale in bygone years. It was this typical London clay that was used in the potteries of Notting Dale to produce the bricks that found their way into so many of the buildings erected during the house-building boom of the early- to mid-nineteenth century.

The other major geographical feature of the area is, or rather was in the past, the rivers – and well may you say 'what rivers?' The two rivers that at one time ran through Notting Hill were the Westbourne and Counters Creek. The Westbourne rises in Hampstead and runs through the borough in the Westbourne Grove area. It continues on to Kensington Gardens where it feeds the Serpentine before heading for Knightsbridge and Sloane Square. If you look up while waiting for an underground train at Sloane

Square you will notice a huge iron pipe crossing the line at a high level – it contains the Westbourne. The outfall of the Westbourne is into the Thames near the eastern end of the Chelsea Hospital gardens. The river has been fully enclosed since about the mid-1850s and it now forms the Ranelagh sewer. The name Westbourne was originally the name of the area, not the river – the meaning of the name being 'west of the bourne', with 'bourne' being an old word for a stream or river. In addition to giving its name to the Westbourne part of North Kensington it also gave the name of Knightsbridge to that area of the borough. It is alleged that two knights fought to the death on a bridge over the Westbourne to the south of were Kensington Gardens are today.

The other river of North Kensington is Counters Creek, which rises near the Kensal Green Cemetery. From there it runs in an almost straight line in a southerly direction, passing close by the old White City and on to Olympia, Earls Court and its outfall into the Chelsea stretch of the Thames. It gets its name from an old bridge that crossed the river in the Earls Court area, supposedly owned by the Countess of Oxford who owned the area at the time. The name therefore could be a corruption of 'Countesses Bridge', which first appeared in 1421 as 'Contessebregge'.

Industry within the area has changed over the centuries, being solely made up of arable farming up until the late-eighteenth century when the manufacture of bricks and pottery was started in Notting Dale. Pig farming soon followed in the Latimer Road area, which was in close proximity to the kilns of the potteries. The area was known for many years as a 'bag, bottle and bone district', which refers to the occupations carried out by many of its inhabitants, virtually all of whom were extremely poor. They made their money by collecting and sorting through rubbish. Another less-than-pleasant way of making money was collecting dogs' droppings, which were used in the leather-tannin industry. It appears that virtually all the occupations practiced in the Dale during the early to middle 1800s were unpleasant, physically hard and financially unrewarding.

The retail trade has, for almost one and a half centuries, been well represented by both shops and the markets full of costermongers, a tradition that has both survived and indeed proliferated. Even the motor-manufacturing trade has been represented in the west of the borough with the Sunbeam Talbot motor company having a facility (formerly the Clement Talbot Works) in the Barlby Road area. The motor works were located just east of another large employer in the area – 'The Gas Light and Coke Company' was to be found between the GWR and the canal. Its gasometers (gas-storage tanks) towered over everything else for miles around.

On the other side of the canal was another employer and indeed an area of tranquillity in this now-industrialised part of the borough – the Kensal

Green Cemetery, a large purpose-built cemetery serving London's deceased.

In 2006 the employment needs of the area are serviced by the retail trade, entertainment and tourism, and financial and service institutions. Within the borough can be found names such as the Virgin Group (which was indeed founded in Vernon Yard, Portobello Road), Island Records, Rough Trade Records, the Trevor Horne Organisation, Chrysalis and a whole lot more. North Kensington is a particularly well-used set for films and television programmes, and reached new realms of fame with the 1999 film *Notting Hill*, when it actually became one of the stars. The streets are featured in numerous productions and its buildings, being so recognisable, are seen on a regular basis. The old Rootes Hall (formerly the Clement Talbot Works) was for a time also a studio for the Thames Television Company.

Religion has proved a strong and enduring force in this borough. Throughout the centuries we have seen churches, synagogues, chapels, monasteries and convents in various locations, with many of their buildings and organisations remaining to look after the spiritual wellbeing of the inhabitants of this part of West London.

The Labour Member of Parliament for Regent's Park and North Kensington, Karen Buck. 'As MP for the area I welcome celebration of the local community as in this book.'

A No. 28 'Routemaster' bus at Notting Hill in 1987.

London

With it's Buckingham Palace
Beefeaters and Gin
Parliament house
And houses of sin
Harrods and Soho
The locals and tourists
A wealth of museums
For those that are purists

London's a city
For young and for old
With welcoming arms
Come in from the cold
A big melting-pot
Of culture and races
The city's alive
A huge sea of faces

Catch a show
Visit markets
Or just stand and stare
But beware of the pigeons
In Trafalgar Square
Such a beautiful city
By day and by night
Full of people and voices
Laughter and light

London gets in your blood
Right from the start
Takes hold and moves in
To a place in your heart

Debbie Strawbridge, exiled in Australia.
Debbie has been in Australia since she was a child,
but from her poem we can tell that she, as with anyone else that
comes from or just visits London, it is in her blood.

Above: *Notting Barns Farm in the mid-1800s.*

Below: *Porto Bello Farm as it was in 1864, in a picture by D. Strawbridge.*

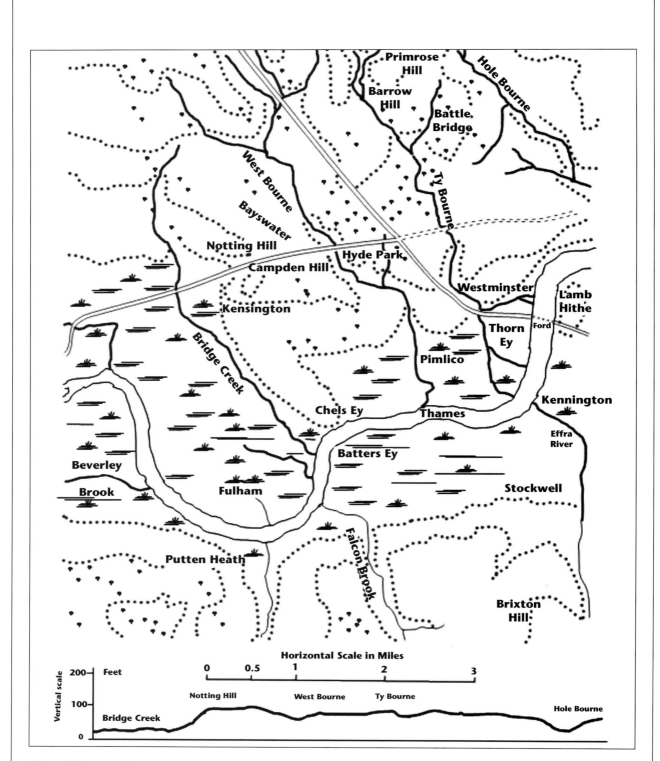

Map of West London in Roman times with some of the important features given their early names. Note Counters Creek has the name Bridge Creek.

(REDRAWN BY M. WILKINSON)

Notting Hill, London West 11, From Farmyard Chick to Urban Chic

The name Notting Hill (or associated names) can be traced back to about 700AD, but it is known that the Romans where also familiar with the area. Roman roads cut across the area, through the densely wooded country and heading for Londinium. The route of the Roman roads are represented by modern roads, with the Edgware Road running where once Watlin Street would have carried the occupying forces to and from the capital. That, however, is not the beginning, for where the Romans built their highways the early British made trackways for the Trinobantes to make their way to their principal settlement in what is now Colchester.

Chenesitun was a village made up of just a few buildings. It was founded by Saxon families, new immigrants, but the name of the settlement is probably the early form of Kensington. Other parts of the area also got familiar names about this time – near to Watlin Street a clan known as the Poedings or 'sons of Padda' settled, probably close to where Paddington is today. Not far away yet another Saxon family, the Cnottingas or 'sons of Cnotta', settled on a raised terrace, now known as Notting Hill. The Saxon origins of Kensington and its politically joined neighbour of Chelsea are both mentioned in the Domesday Book of 1086, at the time the manor of Kensington was owned by Aubrey de Vere. The de Vere family owned the manor of Kensington for some five centuries and, as lords of the manor, were answerable only to the monarch on civil matters appertaining to the manor and its inhabitants.

Later on Notting Hill went from being a stretch of woodland in the county of Middlesex to a landscape of meadows and fields, to what it became in the Victorian period – a bustling part of a busy capital city into which people would flood from all over England and indeed the world.

In 1543 the meadow and farm land was seized by Henry VIII, but due the fact that he died in 1547 there is little possibility that he even visited his acquisition.

With all the history in the locality it's difficult to decide when and how Notting Hill as we know it was fashioned. So let's concentrate on the period from the 1800s to the present day, as it was during this period that the character of the area was defined and Notting Hill became a residential district.

The area we now know as Notting Hill is located in North Kensington and has undergone vast changes in the last 200 years – it has gone from a two-farm patch of arable land to a busy, vibrant and exciting part of one of the great, if not the greatest, capital cities in the world.

As the 1700s turned into the 1800s practically all that made up the area were a few humble dwellings and the two farms – Porto Bello Farm, comprising of some 400 acres of cornfields and meadow land, and Notting Barns Farm, occupying a smaller plot of about 150 acres, mainly turned over to dairy farming. With the expansion of residential and retail developments in the mid-1800s the life of the two farms was limited with Porto Bello Farm being sold off in 1866 and Notting Barns Farm following a similar fate in 1880.

The borough grew outwards from Holland Park in the south and Paddington in the east and reflected the fashion for London squares that were particularly popular in the early- and mid-nineteenth centuries. The road we now know as Notting Hill Gate has run its route since Roman times – it was the main route from London to Silchester. It was later a road that was notorious for highwaymen, intoxicated highwaymen in the main because, for a long time, there was very little along the road apart from coaching inns and gravel pits. The present name is derived from the old toll-gate that was located in the hamlet, which was established in the eighteenth century and was particularly resented by the inhabitants of the area. By the mid-1800s the developers had moved in and rows of low terraced housing sprang up to the south of the toll-gate, funded by early developers.

The Grand Junction Canal at Ladbroke Grove, with the Dissenters Chapel of Kensal Green Cemetery pictured on the left, December 2005.

Kensal Green Cemetery in the winter of 2005.

However, it was noted by the local vicar that 'the alleys and yards are foul and the inhabitants poorer than any in the East End.'

Developers continued to build and the spread of construction continued in a westerly direction along Notting Hill Gate. As these populated areas spread the need for shops, services and transport increased. This brought about changes in some of the thoroughfares, such as Portobello Road, which stretched northward and attracted many foreign migrants. Such was the success of Portobello Road that migrants came from many different parts of the world. Portobello Road became a trading centre from very early on.

From my first memory of Notting Hill I have known Portobello Road as 'the Lane'. It is a throw-back from when the road was no more than a farm track running from Kensington Gravel Pits through to Kensal Village. At this time the track was known as Porto Bello Lane. Towards the northern end was Porto Bello Farm with Notting Barns off to the west. The name Porto Bello is derived from the Battle of Puerto Bello fought in 1739, which left the British with a great sense of pride and excitement. It was Admiral Sir Edward Vernon (who was also an MP and carried the nickname 'Old Grog') that captured the Caribbean port, commanding a flotilla of six British Navy ships. Vernon had been sent to the Antilles to harry the Spanish during the curiously named 'War of Jerkin's Ear'. The battle caught the imagination of the public, which led to the names Porto Bello and Vernon turning up on alehouses, roads and towns throughout the land. Over time 'Porto Bello' was corrupted into the more familiar 'Portobello'.

The name of Vernon, or should I say his nick-name, was also to go down in history for yet another reason. In 1740 he issued the order that the rum ration given to sailors was to be diluted with water – from that time on the mixture was known as 'grog'.

To the west of the borough the Paddington branch of the Grand Junction Canal pushes towards the heart of London. The canal was the prime means of transporting goods from the industrial heartland of the Midlands. Bricks would be transported by the then-horsedrawn or steam barges, destined for the

Kensal Green Cemetery with the Western Gas Company's gasometers in the background, 2005.

building sites of Kensington, Chelsea and other growing boroughs of an expanding capital city. The canal was opened to traffic on 1 June 1801 and crosses the northern end of Portobello Lane, following a rough line parallel to Harrow Road and on to the Paddington basin.

In 1833 the first purpose-built cemetery for London was located to the north of the canal at Kensal Green. A total of almost 60 acres was set aside as a response to the shocking overcrowding of London's church graveyards. So bad was the situation that the rich could purchase graves already occupied and have the interred bodies removed. Those removed were very often unceremoniously disposed of in the local rivers or watercourses.

In the area enclosed by the Grand Junction Canal and Great Western Railway was Kensal New Town which was built in the 1840s. The new town was made up of rows of cottages with front and rear gardens. Employment was mainly supplied by the Western Gas Company and Kensal Green Cemetery. The women were primarily engaged in laundry work which led to the area gaining the nickname 'Soapsuds Island'. Kensal New Town, with its overcrowding, pollution and industrialisation, soon degenerated into a slum, an area which by its very location and nature was left to its own devices. It was only charities that attempted to alleviate the social and health problems that plagued the community. The turn of the nineteenth

The Clement Talbot works in the 1930s, with a display of new London County Council ambulances. This must have been a time when blocking a highway for a photo shoot was acceptable. Note also the gasometer of the Western Gas Company, just visible over the main building.

Carts loaded with coke at the Western Gas Company's Kensal Gasworks in 1909. (COURTESY OF NATIONAL GRID)

century saw responsibility for this sad and over-crowded community given to the newly formed Royal Borough of Kensington.

Parts of the area of North Kensington, namely Notting Dale, became known as the 'Potteries and Piggeries'. The Potteries were populated by workers from the brick and pottery works. Bricks were in great demand because of the amount of building going on in London, which led to kilns and chimneys becoming a familiar part of the landscape – the last of these kilns is located in Walmer Road.

The Piggeries were so named because of the sheer volume of pigs being reared there. Gypsies and travellers began to populate these areas and slum dwellings and caravan camps sprang up. Over time, levels of crime and disease in these districts got out of hand.

In 1867 the population of the areas was to be supplemented by the poor from the seemingly more-affluent part of the borough. Just off High Street Kensington the 'secret slums' could be found. They consisted of a number of yards with associated dwellings, namely Market Court, Browns Buildings, Gardeners Buildings and the notorious Jennings Buildings. Jennings Buildings alone housed some 1,500 souls – mainly Irish labourers who worked in the market gardens of the area and later on the building sites. The conditions in these slums were appalling and by 1867 a slum-clearance programme swept them away, leaving the residents to find accommodation elsewhere. The Potteries and Piggeries of Notting Dale offered the only suitable relocation option for many of these people.

The question that I hope to answer in this section is 'what came first, Potteries or Piggeries?'.

In 1781 James Watson purchased 17 acres of land to the north of the Norland estate. The soil of this land was made almost entirely of the London clay that is used for London stock bricks. The brickfields were not only confined to the area around Walmer

Road. By the very nature of the land's make-up, suitable clay could be found all around, so inevitably brickfields could also to be found in White City and North Pole Road, amongst other places. By the early-nineteenth century there were only a few buildings on the land and the brickfields, as they were now known, had been split up and sold to new owners – namely Samuel Lake and William Adams. Adams Brickfield was a business that lasted for many years and it is believed that he also founded the 'Norland Pottery Works' in Walmer Road, which made tiles, pots and drainpipes. It is to these works that the last remaining bottle kiln belonged, which stands protected in Walmer Road. This area was particularly run down and on the site of Avondale Park a vast body of putrid stagnant water known as the 'Ocean' was located. It was the result of clay workings associated with the potteries. The area of the Piggeries and Potteries was hit by a devastating outbreak of cholera in 1848 – such was the severity of the outbreak that the authorities, namely the commissioners of sewers, were forced into action. However, the action was too little to make any major difference. It is worthwhile noting that, at the time, the pigs of the area outnumbered the humans, and the infant mortality rate was running at more than 50 per cent. Poverty was so bad that it was only matched by one or two areas located in the East End of London. Medical help was only available to those who could afford it (which was no one in the locality), or those who could access that which was provided on a charitable basis.

Samuel Lake is also associated with the beginnings of the Piggeries, because it was he who sold

Wilsham Street was amongst the poorest streets of Notting Dale. Today the street is clean and tidy and the houses well maintained, as revealed in this 2005 photograph.

The preserved kiln in the Potteries area of Notting Dale, viewed from Walmer Road.

Erno Goldfinger's Trellick Tower and Golborne Road.

part of his land in 1820 to a gentleman named Stephens for £100, in order that he might keep pigs. Stephens was acquainted with pig keepers from what is now the Connaught Square part of London – a part of London that was soon to be developed into a residential area. Being situated on land that was soon to be turned into up-market housing for the gentry, the pig keepers sought a new location for their animals and families. The pig masters of the 'West End Establishment', as they called themselves, either purchased or rented plots of land from Stephens and set up their new smallholdings on parts of the brickfield site. Therefore, it can be deduced that the Potteries came before the Piggeries.

In the early part of the twentieth century the Potteries and Piggeries were finally cleared and many of the displaced residents moved northwards to the Golborne and Kensal areas of North Kensington. Unfortunately they moved from one overcrowded slum to another. In the 1920s it was recorded that in one street in that district '140 houses contained 2,500 inhabitants'. The conditions didn't change much until the 1960s, when serious slum clearance led to large numbers of dwellings being emptied and demolished. The resulting urban regeneration led to large developments such as Trellick Tower, a typical late-1960s concrete tower block in the Golborne area.

In terms of failed or unusual ventures, probably one of the most amazing facts is that in 1836 Mr J. Whyte obtained some 2,000 acres of land bounded by Portobello Lane, Notting Barns Farm and Notting Hill. The purpose of this land? A racecourse. Unfortunately the life of the Hippodrome, as it was called, was short-lived – less than five years. The racecourse opened on 3 June 1837 but almost immediately problems caused a rethink of the project. A public footpath running from north to south crossed the racecourse. The footpath was being used by many people avoiding crossing the Kensington Potteries. It can be no accident that during this period Pottery Lane picked up the nickname 'Cut Throat Lane'. During the opening of the course a crowd of some 1,000 broke down the barriers baring their passage over the hill within the racecourse. Of the 12,000 to 14,000 spectators that day, the majority probably gained free access. By 17 June Mr Whyte had again blocked access to the footpath with piles of earth and rubble, but opposition was such that local inhabitants, councillors and labourers, duly accompanied by the police, arrived to clear the barricade, again giving free access to the hill and the rest of the racecourse. The free access was exploited by thieves, hawkers and gypsies who used the opportunity to mingle with the gentry and race-going fraternity. As a last-ditched effort to save his project, the following year Mr Whyte fenced off the footpath, which again failed to solve his problem. At this point Mr Whyte gave up the eastern end of the Hippodrome and remodelled his racecourse so it was not cut through by the right of way. Even following the problems and resolutions of the previous seasons the racecourse fell foul of yet another show-stopper. This problem was the make-up of the land on which the racecourse was established. It is not that the land was special in any way, in fact it was the same as most of London – clay, the raw material that went into the local potteries for brickmaking. The clay-rich soil turned into a quagmire at the first hint of water and would then not drain for an age. The last race to be held at the Hippodrome was a steeplechase on 2 June 1841 – virtually four years to the day after opening.

The fabulous Brunel-designed station at Paddington was the terminus for his Great Western Railway. The main line passes through the borough at the northern end of Portobello Lane and Ladbroke Grove, and follows adjacent to Wornington Road to Westbourne Park then on to Royal Oak and Paddington. The line was completed in 1838 and was serviced by steam trains right through to the late 1960s, when diesel and electricity took over.

Notting Hill was still developing and by the 1870s the roads of elegant Victorian houses had stretched as far north as Elgin Crescent on Portobello Lane and in the east to All Saints Church. Shepherd's Bush was also expanding to meet Notting Dale in the west.

The Nunney Castle *at the eastern terminus of the Great Western Railway, Brunel's magnificent Paddington Station, 2001.*

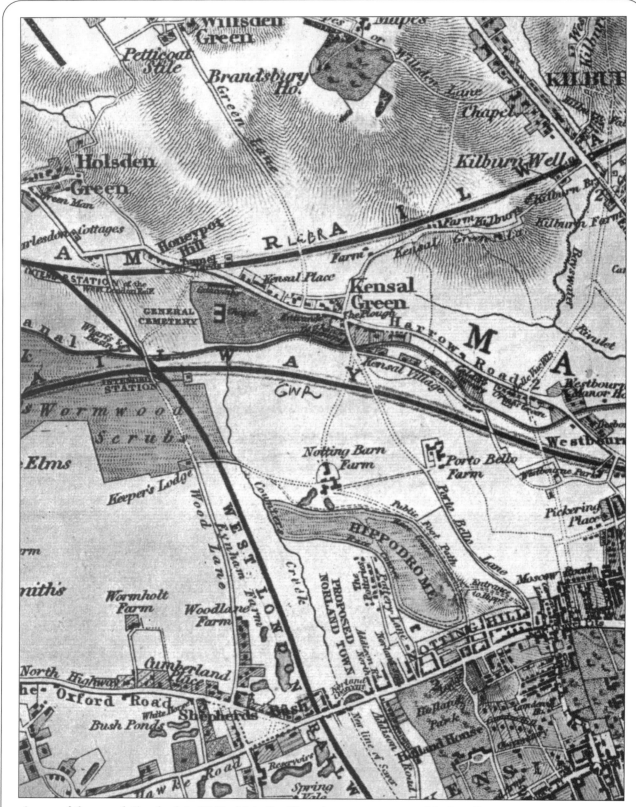

A map of the area dating back to 1841. Note the Hippodrome racecourse with the adjacent area for the proposed Norland Town.

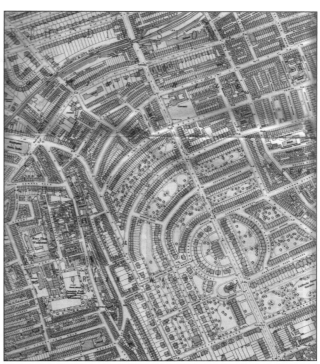

A map from the mid-1800s showing open fields and few dwellings north of Elgin Crescent. The shape of the Ladbroke, Kensington Park and Norland estates can clearly be seen developing.

By the early 1900s the spread of houses in the area was virtually complete, indicating the speed at which developers worked.

Fields could still be seen around Ladbroke Grove Station, stretching as far as Kensal Green Cemetery. This agricultural landscape was also hanging on in the Westbourne Grove area, but things were starting to speed up. The catalyst for development was the railway. The Hammersmith and City Railway was completed in 1864 and, with its stations in Ladbroke Road (originally called Notting Hill Station), Latimer Road and Westbourne Park, the die was cast for a development explosion. Houses, shops, schools and churches grew up in the area, and the farms that gave their names to the district disappeared. In 1864 Porto Bello Farm was sold to an order of Catholic nuns who built a convent and home for the aged poor of the area.

Charles Dickens junr wrote of Notting Hill in the *Dickens Dictionary of London* in 1879:

Notting Hill is a comparatively cheap area of London. Here a fair sized house may be had from £75 to £120 according to whether it approaches from the Western or Eastern verge of the district.

As the roads and crescents of Notting Hill grew up, so the individual characters of these village-like communities became embedded. Each had a charm and character of its own with various types of architecture individual to that cluster of roads. Some parts were populated by craftsmen such as bricklayers and carpenters, who worked on building the family homes in Kensington, while others were populated by shopkeepers and costermongers. The architecture

of these areas reflected the trades of the residents – small cobbled mews with stables and living accommodation over for the totters and stallholders, and small cottage-type terraces where other tradesmen would live.

In 1888 the Kensington baths and wash-house on Lancaster Road and Silchester Road were built and remained in operation until the 1970s. The facilities gave much-needed bathing and washing facilities to the many poor families in the area, and it was a clear signal that Notting Hill was coming of age. The baths were such a focal point for the community that I doubt there wasn't a schoolchild in the area that didn't learn to swim there, or a woman that didn't at some point do her washing there. They probably even took their baths in the tiled surroundings of this Victorian waterworld.

Hospitals were another necessity for the inhabitants of North Kensington which were not in as plentiful supply as one would have hoped or needed. The Princess Louise Hospital is one of the older medical establishments in the area. It was built in 1924 by the people of Kensington for the sick children of the area and run by charitable donations and voluntary efforts. It is a hospital that I look back on fondly as its name for some reason made it seem less frightening than, say, the Hammersmith Hospital. It is only recently that I have learned the reason for its name, and indeed about the patron herself. The hospital, although built in 1924, is based on work dating back to the early- to mid-nine-

St Lukes Mews, the former totters' dwellings, now boast roof gardens.

Lansdowne Crescent from Ladbroke Grove.

Left: *Artisan cottages in Portobello Road, the former home of George Orwell.*

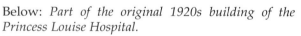

Below: *Part of the original 1920s building of the Princess Louise Hospital.*

LONDON SCHOOLS'
SWIMMING ASSOCIATION

FIRST CLASS CERTIFICATE

awarded to

Melvin Wilkinson.

for swimming One Hundred yards

Date.. *12. 11. 64*

Swimming certificate for 100 yards gained at the Lancaster Road swimming-baths in 1964.

The Victorian façade of Buckingham Terrace School, now renamed Colville Junior School.

teenth century when local doctors founded a medical dispensary in Kensington. It was a time of hardship and poverty with a workhouse system in operation. Medical care was expensive and rarely available for the lower classes. By 1900 a new children's ward was added but consisted of a mere 11 beds. The hospital was in its more permanent premises between 1847 and 1925. It was late in the nineteenth century that the population of Kensington changed, with the poorer working-class residents moving out towards the newer parts of North Kensington. The Potteries, Piggeries and Notting Dale were, as described previously, the poorest areas, but with a rising population reaching some 26,000 souls. It is a sad and indeed shameful fact that the infant mortality rate of these areas was twice that of the more affluent parts of Kensington – of the children born in the area 50 per cent did not make it past five years of age; an astonishing statistic for a civilised country in the late 1800s. With the Kensington Dispensary located in the wrong (southern) part of Kensington, something needed to be done to relocate these valuable medical facilities nearer to the poorer (northern) parts of the borough.

With both extreme wealth and poverty found in the borough it was hoped that funds for building new premises for the dispensary could be raised by charitable contributions from the wealthy. Princess Louise was the daughter of Queen Victoria, who took personal control of fund-raising and organising the setting up of a new children's hospital in North Kensington. She was the president of the Kensington Dispensary, as indeed her husband, the Duke of Argyll, had been before her. She raised the £80,000 needed and the hospital was built over four years, with its opening in 1928 following completion of the project.

During the Second World War the hospital was damaged three times by German bombs, but it remained open throughout, maintaining full service. The hospital continued to be run on a voluntary basis until 1948, when the National Health Service took control.

Schooling in the borough was provided mainly by charity or church schools such as the 'ragged schools' and various missions. ('Ragged schools' were funded by wealthy individuals to educate poor children without charging a fee. They were often also engaged in social welfare activities.) These establishments would have been set up by wealthy benefactors, churches or other educational organisations. It was in 1870 that the Education Act allowed for funds to be raised from local rates to provide buildings and cover running costs of educational establishments.

Amongst the first to be established was Buckingham Terrace School which opened in 1875. The school is still in operation in 2006 with the new name of Colville Junior School – an educational establishment that, I am proud to say, I and my sister attended.

The Second World War brought more hardships to the area and is remembered by Eddie Adams elsewhere in this book. The area was ravaged by air raids during the Blitz, and also felt the devastating power of the doodlebugs (the German V2 rockets). It was a terrible and trying time for all its inhabitants and as the air raids increased in intensity and frequency many of the local children were evacuated to the relative safety of rural areas. Those remaining in the borough tended to be the women, those men in reserved occupations and the elderly. The Land Army

Land Army girls in Wiltshire during the Second World War. The girls came from all over the country, including London, Liverpoool and Manchester. Jessie Coward is in the middle row, far left.

girls were sent out to various parts of the countryside to work on farms, and became a band of sisters bonded together by their determination to keep the British public fed. Farms that had been worked by the rural men were now enlivened by the sound of young women doing this hard manual work.

The damage and casualties in the area were extensive with some 3,000 casualties and 33,000 houses destroyed, including the beautiful and historic Holland House. The remains of the property were purchased by the LCC in 1952 and its grounds opened as a public park, now known as Holland Park.

The area around Portobello Road had always been populated by the working class, but following the Second World War times were hard. There was a shortage of employment and decent affordable housing – it was not an area that needed or could easily sustain an influx of residents. However, by the late 1940s and early 1950s the population was being swollen by migrants from the Caribbean. The 'Empire Windrush' immigrants, amongst others, arrived in Britain and found their way to Notting Hill, but it was not to be the heaven they had been expecting. They had the same problems as existing residents – poor housing, extortionate rents, unscrupulous landlords and poor employment potential – but their problems went even deeper. Racism was rife and by the late 1950s race riots erupted on the streets of Notting Hill. The disturbances were a magnet for those young whites that wanted to seek out trouble and for the black community who needed to protect themselves, their families and their property. The young white 'Teddy boy' and motorcycle gangs would pick on the local Afro-Caribbean community until almost inevitably they stood up for themselves with violent consequences. Young black males such as Michael de Freitas, later to be known as Michael X, Frank Crichlow and Baron Baker made a stand at a West Indian café in Blenheim Crescent. They fought off a

white mob that had descended on the area. Frank Crichlow later went on to run 'The Mangrove' café on All Saints Road – another café which would go down in black folklore in Notting Hill. The Notting Hill race riots are a dark part of London W11's history but a part that is still remembered clearly by those of us who lived through them.

Being a hotbed of racism made the area a fertile recruiting ground for the likes of Oswald Mosley and his 'brown-shirt thugs'. I can clearly remember a Mosley rally taking place in All Saints Road – it was in 1958. Mosley would use a flatbed lorry as a makeshift platform. Although only five years old at the time, I can remember the situation, if not the words of hatred. In 1959, following the racist murder of young Antiguan Kelso Cochrane, an act too far for both communities, and one that at last would bring the communities closer, Mosley and his union movement stood for parliament. However, the fascist doctrine of his union party was falling on deaf ears, as by now Notting Hill was a multi-racial community with no place for his kind of politics. It became apparent that many members of the community, both black and white, were suffering similar hardships. What the area needed was what we now call 'urban development'. The residents set up help groups concentrating on housing problems, racism and the lack of employment, and there was no shortage of MPs beating on doors with promises of urban renewal – all they needed was the votes of the needy. In the early part of the 1960s Pearl Jephcott, an experienced social investigator, wrote *A Troubled Area* which looked critically at the causes of the riots in Notting Hill. She pointedly noted:

... the riots of 1958 brought Notting Hill into the limelight as a district where people came to live because they had to and left as soon as possible because they wanted to.

Things changed throughout the 1960s and '70s, with Notting Hill becoming an area where people wanted to live, but with the programmes of urban renewal many were forced to leave. As the 1980s and '90s arrived the incoming population just stayed because they loved the area.

If the 1950s go down as a low point in the history of Notting Hill, then the 1960s are a high spot in the local history. It has been said that if you can remember the '60s you weren't there – well maybe I was at an age that meant I was old enough to see and remember the '60s era in Notting Hill, but young enough not to have experienced some of the excesses of that decade.

But what was it like living here in the '60s? In the parlance of the time 'it was fab', especially in Portobello Road. The Lane, as we knew, it became very fashionable in the early '60s, with the beautiful people of the hippy age descending on the area for second-hand clothes, pop art paraphernalia, music and certain mind-altering substances. There is one particular shop that I remember very well – 'I was Lord Kitchener's Valet' was, for want of a better word, a boutique that sold all types of Victorian military dress uniforms. It was a commodity which the average business person would clearly avoid like the plague if he wanted to sell them in volume to the general public. How wrong can you be – every hip and modern trendsetter in the country wanted the typically red tunic jackets or black police cape. They became so popular that pop stars bought them up on a massive scale, and even the Beatles and Jimi Hendrix could be seen browsing the racks of clothes in this popular Portobello Road emporium. It was a great regret of mine that at ten years of age I couldn't find one to fit my tiny frame, but then I could never have afforded one anyway. Once they became internationally known the shop was taken to court for a breach of the trades description act – the problem... the proprietors where not valets to Lord Kitchener. After being found guilty and fined the problem was overcome with the addition of the word 'NOT' in the name over the shopfront. 'I was not Lord Kitchener's Valet' carried on trading for a long time afterwards and, as new fashions such as Afghan coats and caftans became popular, the shop simply added these to their stock. I can still smell the patchouli oil and incense that seemed to hang in the air of the shop, and indeed up and down Portobello Road.

As children living close to and going to school in Portobello Road, my sister and I and our friends would find ways to earn pocket money from the market. I can remember my sister disappearing off to the Lane with a box of old toys and things one Saturday morning with a plan to make some spending money for a school trip to Marchants Hill school camp. She had scrounged an old orange box (in those days they were fairly sturdy and made of wood) and set up a stall on the corner of Lancaster Road and Portobello Road, and was selling her wares. The local constabulary was not amused and my sister was marched home by the policeman. Unfortunately for him Dot Wilkinson, my mother, was a typical W11 mother and housewife and the unsuspecting PC got short shrift from her. However, once she had finished with the poor young police officer my sister got the rough end of her tongue. Personally I didn't want to suffer my mother's anger so I found less conspicuous ways of earning money. I would go to the café for the stallholders to collect their pots of tea, an errand for which you could expect a few coppers (pennies) or a tanner (sixpence). Now and again, as we got bigger, some of us would help on the stalls, emptying the fruit and veg from the boxes or other chores to earn half a crown (2s.6d. or 12½ pence in today's money) or a couple of bob (a florin or 2s., or 10 pence today). I really enjoyed it and occasionally there was a little excitement if someone was caught stealing, or you found a large spider in the big orange-coloured wooden crates the bananas were packed into. The

stallholders always had something comical to say to their customers, especially as at that time 99 per cent of them were housewives, and the young men on the stalls would flirt like mad.

It was a fantastic atmosphere and provided a lesson in life that you could never learn in a classroom. I feel lucky and privileged to have had this type of education and have carried some of the things I learnt though my life. The trouble was that it was an education that was interrupted during weekdays by schooling at Colville Junior Mixed School.

The Royal Borough of Kensington and Chelsea has had royal connections since the sixteenth century, but 1689 was when it had its first royal resident, when William III took up residence in Kensington Palace. It is a royal home that has been in use ever since and indeed saw the birth of Queen Victoria in 1819. She remained in Kensington Palace until her accession to the thrown in 1837.

The population of Kensington has increased dramatically over the last 200 years and during the period of 30 years from 1801–31 records show that it increased from 8,500 souls to 20,902, and remained the smaller neighbour of Chelsea until the outward spread of the borough extended to Notting Barns. It was in 1861 that Kensington officially became the greater in population of the two boroughs. In 2006 the twin boroughs have a joint population of around 180,000.

London W11 is well known to have a split personality, with the wealthy, rich and famous living in close proximity to the poor and needy. The chic areas were sought after and expensive, while the poorer parts were run down and shabby. One such run-down area was All Saints Road, which was home for me and my family during the 1950s and '60s. During the 1980s it was a road that had become known as the 'front line', a road where people lived in fear and which police were wary to patrol. The drug dealing hit such proportions that it was like a narcotics supermarket. Frequent drug raids did little or nothing to solve the problem and accusations of police intimidation meant that relationships between the community and police were at an all-time low. In 1987 the then deputy divisional commander for Notting Hill, Ian Hutchison, launched 'Operation Trident' in an effort to, in his words, 'regain control of the streets'. Despite continuing accusations of police harassment by young black members of the community the operation started to win over the majority of residents, who began to see improvements in the safety of the borough's streets and a rejuvenation of the area. A Notting Hill address became much sought after and the neighbourhood atmosphere was fast growing into one of peace and harmony. Restaurants, wine bars and businesses started moving into the area, further enhancing the community spirit. It became a place to eat out, a place for families to live and a place to visit.

Above: *Blenheim Crescent with its fabulous restored properties.*

Left: *The lower end of Lancaster Road, now painted and renovated.*

Chepstow Villas near the junction with Portobello Road.

Chapter 2

The Architectural Heritage of Our Part of London

If you ask people what style of architecture or buildings are typical of Notting Hill most would probably say the Victorian London squares, terraces and crescents, such as Colville Square and Lansdowne Crescent. They are indeed beautiful with their three- and four-storey dwellings that have had chequered lives. They started out as family homes for the wealthy, people that commuted into the city of London via the new railway systems and bus services, and titled and successful business people that wanted to live away from the busy city centre. However, it was a problem that the volume of buildings would mean purchasers

Alfred Wilkinson in the Co-op butchers in Westbourne Park Road, c.1965.

were at a premium and many remained empty or became multi-family dwellings. These large houses and villas started falling into disrepair as Notting Hill became a less desirable part of London for the rich, and the now-vacant and shabby buildings lent themselves to being converted into flats and multi-occupancy dwellings for working-class families, with many being converted into bedsits or low-cost accommodation for the ever-changing population of the borough. It became known for a long time as 'bedsit land', with young singles and migrant workers moving in and out. Many of these large houses fell into disrepair as unscrupulous or uncaring landlords failed to maintain them properly. Speculators started to buy them up, and squatters and communes moved into others, especially in the flower-power and hippy days of the 1960s and '70s. All of this took its toll on the noble edifices.

In the late-twentieth and early-twenty-first century these buildings have seen a resurgence of popularity and have had new life breathed into them. They have been renovated to their former glory with clean white, sky-blue or even pink painted façades and large communal gardens. Basement apartments and penthouses are popular and have attracted the rich and famous back to Notting Hill. The grand houses again stand proud and magnificent, and it would seem appropriate for horse-drawn hackney carriages to pick up gentlemen in top hats and ladies with ball gowns. However, time has moved on so it is black cabs and BMWs with no manure for the roses.

If you walk around the area you will find that many of the large town houses have blue plaques on them, which indicates that at some point in the building's history an interesting, important or famous person has had a connection with it. The fact that

there are so many plaques indicates the importance of the area in earlier years and its popularity as a borough to live in to this day.

Although, as I have said, the Victorian terraces are indeed imposing and obvious candidates for the face of Notting Hill, there are many worthy and important individual dwellings within the borough. Many of these are owner accommodation for shops or businesses. The premises may also have been used by business owners as tied accommodation for staff, or used as rented accommodation to generate income. To fully appreciate these architectural gems we need to raise our field of view above the shop fronts and explore the façades of the upper floors. As a child I was brought up above a shop, as my father was a butcher by trade, having left the Army after the war. He studied at night school and became a butcher for the London Co-operative Society (LCS), or the Co-op as it was known. We lived next door to, and later above, the Co-op in Westbourne Park Road. The Co-op had two parts – it had a kind of supermarket section (before supermarkets where large and out of town) and a butcher's shop next door. I remember that the butcher's shop had marble-topped window display counters and the floor was covered in sawdust. (This was always handy because, as a child, I kept white mice and the free sawdust was great for their bedding.) The front of the shop had ceramic tiles on the outside and in the early days the windows would open like a sash

No. 234 Westbourne Park Road, formerly the London Co-operative Society shop and meeting hall. The flat above was a tied property for Co-op employees.

Melvin Wilkinson, Alison Uphill and Keith Smith on the flat roof area above the Co-op shop in 1960. The buildings behind are in All Saints Road.

All Saints Road in the early 1900s. The buildings on the left are those seen in the background of the other picture (left).

window, to allow an enhanced display of the produce. The general provisions section was very similar and also had marble interior fittings, but had tiled floors. I can even remember my mother's dividend number, which was 458769 – funny what you can remember! But I digress. Back to the accommodation above the shop. On the first floor was a meeting hall which was used by, amongst others, the Jehovah's Witnesses, who used it for meetings on a weekly basis. At weekends it was used for weddings and functions. My sister and I were in awe of the sound systems that would arrive for the West Indian weddings. Many where just huge, but in fact the power output was probably quite low compared with sound systems that are used these days at the carnival and other events. As children my sister and I loved it when various bands hired the hall for practice and often wondered if any of the acts made it to the big time and became famous (I guess with the area's history and the volume of bands that used the premises some must have became well known at some point). The windows of the meeting hall and our flat where arched and from the outside

where quite distinctive, making the building look quite imposing, even though the building was only built in a dull-grey brick. The building was topped with a flat roof from which we occasionally watched the streets below. During the race riots of the late 1950s we, along with the residents of the upper floors of Clydesdale House opposite, could see some of the disturbances unfold. However, they are stories for another chapter. As the premises where on the corner they adjoined No. 1 All Saints Road and between the two premises and above the Co-op was a balcony or flat-roof section which was a playground for me, my sister and our friends. This flat roof has since been built on and has become another residence.

Along the Portobello Road and further along All Saints Road are some fabulous buildings, and again you need to raise you gaze above shop level to catch a glimpse of these architectural gems. Many of the entrances to these upper-floor dwellings are set between the shops, but no-one really notices them. As you walk along take a look between any of the green-grocers or the ethnic art shops and, yes, that is a front

The Castle, formerly the Warwick Castle, on the corner of Westbourne Park Road It was known as a busman's pub, as they would stop to use the facilities and would often avail themselves of a liquid refreshment as well.

The Kensington Park on Ladbroke Grove, just one of the numerous pubs in the area.

Above: *No. 5 All Saints Road on the corner of St Lukes Mews.*

Above right: *No. 221 Portobello Road. The building to the left is No. 223, which is said to be one of the oldest buildings in Portobello Road. The original section of the building is set back with the shop part being a modern addition.*

Right: *The Bramley Arms during the 1958 race riots.*

The Market Bar, which was formerly known as the Golden Cross, on the corner of Lancaster and Portobello Roads.

The Portobello Star.

Above left: *The former Bramley Arms public house in Notting Dale is a local landmark that has been seen in numerous films over the years.*

Above: *Inside the Ground Floor Bar on Portobello Road.*

Left: *Inside the Duke of Wellington public house.*

The Sun in Splendour was built in 1850 at the top of Portobello Road. At one time the pub boasted a huge gold-coloured rising sun, mounted high on the façade.

The Walmer Castle on Ledbury Road.

The old kiln in Walmer Road, at the heart of the Potteries, viewed from Hippodrome Mews.

The main entrance of the Clement Talbot Motor Works, known as Ladbroke Hall and later Rootes Hall.

door. It's funny how, when you see these things on a daily basis, you don't actually notice them.

Many of the residents of the area took a keen interest in the local hostelries. This can be demonstrated in the fact that, even with so many being converted to other uses or being demolished to make way for new housing or businesses, we still direct people around the area by pub name. For example, 'Oh yes you want to go down here to the Apollo, turn left until you reach the Tavistock Arms'. It is nice to notice that many of the pubs have maintained a local and friendly atmosphere. If I were to list all the pubs in the area I could write a book on that subject alone, but instead I shall let the pictures speak for themselves.

Many of the public buildings are also architecturally important, and the mind immediately turns to the fabulous churches and chapels that have attracted worshippers for almost two centuries. The religious buildings of Notting Hill are so rich in character and beauty that I have decided to devote an entire chapter to them, later in this book.

So, what of the industrial buildings of Notting Hill? As far as industrial history is concerned, the last notable examples where probably the Potteries, which were located towards the west of the borough with the last of the kilns being in Walmer Road. The preserved kiln stands opposite Avondale Park, a former flooded claypit. This is the heart of the Potteries but has now given way to mews houses and low-rise accommodation.

Barlby Road is home to the Pall Mall Depository,

a huge building of dark brick and square lines. So proud were Pall Mall of their name that, high up on the building in ceramic brick, the name is spelt out in letters that are around two metres high. The building has been split up into smaller units but its outward appearance remains pretty much intact. Opposite the Pall Mall Depository stands Ladbroke Hall, the former head office and frontage of the Talbot Motor Company. It comes as a bit of a surprise to many that North Kensington had a motor industry, but it did. The historical details of the industry can be found within its own chapter later in the book. The hall has gone through a number of guises – it was initially home to the Talbot Clement Motor Company which became Talbot Darracq and then Sunbeam Talbot Darracq, until Rootes took over the company in the 1930s. After car production finished at 'Rootes Hall' (Ladbroke Hall) the plant was used for a while as a television studio. The production plant at the rear of the hall was later demolished to make way for housing development. The main building remains, externally almost untouched, and doesn't look over 100 years old. The housing estate to the rear maintains the motoring history of the site as the roads are all named after motoring marques associated with either Sunbeam Talbot Darracq (STD) or the Rootes Group. It is also here that we can find probably the only connection with the early history of the area and the old Notting Barns Farm – one small thoroughfare has been given the name Notting Barn Road.

Not far from the location of the motor plant, but on the other side of both the canal and railway, is All Souls Cemetery, so named because the land which was purchased for the purpose of the cemetery was 32 acres of farm land owned by All Souls College Oxford.

Above: *Ladbroke Hall, Barlby Road, in 1905.*

Below: *The reception area of the Clement Talbot Motor Company in 1905. Note the vehicle on display in the centre of the picture.*

It is better known as Kensal Green Cemetery and is a must if we want to look for examples of ornate and exotic architecture. You can effectively travel around the world in this cemetery. Kensal Green Cemetery was created by an act of parliament which gained royal ascent in July 1832, when it became the first of the London Garden cemeteries. The fact that it was a cemetery did not stop the authorities of the time designing what was seen as something of a leisure facility. Its planting and walkways were clearly meant to attract the living into this necropolis and encourage them to linger. It is interesting to read from the early guide which indicates that:

The left-hand road leads to the abodes of the Turks, Jews, Infidels, Heretics and 'unbaptised folk' with the right-hand road after passing among the beautiful and consecrated graves of the faithful, leads to the Episcopal Chapel.

If this was a sales ploy it worked, as within ten years of opening some 6,000 of the departed had been interred within its boundaries.

As indicated the graves, mausoleums, chapels and memorials can be found in styles as diverse as Greek and Gothic, Egyptian to English understated, classic and, for their day, modern. Those interred are from a myriad of backgrounds – indeed one of the most notable is the architect of the industrial age Isambard Kingdom Brunel, whose tracks of the Great Western Railway pass close by his simple and unpresumptuous but solid memorial. Others buried here include royalty in the form of Princess Sophia, daughter of King George III, and her brother Augustus Frederick, Duke of Sussex, as well as writers such as Wilkie Collins and William Makepeace Thackeray, and funambulist extraordinaire Jean Frances Blondin (particularly famous for crossing the Niagara Falls on a tightrope with a man on his back). The cemetery does of course house so many famous and infamous people that it is impossible to name all of them – their memorials and headstones are there to be discovered and admired by the many visitors to the cemetery.

One thing that has occurred during the passing years is that the city has closed in around the acres of calm. What was once a cemetery amongst fields has now become an oasis for wildlife amongst the hustle and bustle of a modern suburb.

The smaller industries or occupations have also left their mark. If you raise your eyes above the street level you will see advertising signs and painted or carved advertisements. One notable example can be seen from the corner of Portobello Road and Westbourne Grove opposite Portobello Court flats and above the antique arcades. Although not strictly an architectural feature, the incised advertisement for 'Mr A. Davey, Builder' is a gem that has survived better than its more modern perspex or paper counterparts. It is worth noting that Mr Davey's business

This road name is the only link with the former farm of Notting Barns. It is on the Barlby Road estate, where virtually all the other roads carry the names of motor car marques, an indication of the area's connection with the motor industry.

was established in 1851, a busy time in the borough for builders, and a time of boom which leaves me wondering if he and his business survived the times of bust.

There is one type of business that was quite big during my early years in London W11, it's distinctive business signs made from brass and steel. The pawnbrokers were all over the area, their signs made up from three brass balls and their windows an Aladdin's cave of gold and silver, anything from wedding rings to silver cutlery, and every item had a story of hardship behind it. Above the shops in the Colville Terrace section of Portobello Road hangs a preserved example of one such pawnbroker's sign and painted wall signage. The shop beneath has, however, long since ceased to be a pawnbroking establishment.

The market traders and totters of the area brought about their own type of architecture in Notting Hill, and the mews houses that are now so desirable were a big part of local living. There are many examples of the mews houses in such locations as St Lukes Mews, Denbigh Mews and Vernon Yard. The mews consisted of terraced buildings with stables underneath (the totters always used horse and carts) and living accommodation above. The dwellings were quite small but in later years, as they became fashionable, loft conversions and roof gardens have been added – notably the stables have been kept and used as garages to house the 4x4 or Mercedes. The road part itself would have been granite cobbled and it is with great pleasure that I can report that most have remained as such, even though in years past the horseshoes and iron-rimmed cartwheels would have made a horrendous noise, usually at four or five in the morning, when the totters went out.

The other tradesmen of the area also lived in typical houses – people such as carpenters, plumbers and builders would usually be found in smaller terraced cottages or houses away from the poorer areas of the Potteries and the more affluent areas of Notting Hill Gate or Kensington. Again, these smaller dwellings have become very desirable and in 2006 can command a high price.

Just one of the splendid mausoleums in Kensal Green Cemetery.

Above: *The incised trade advertisement above the shops in Portobello Road.*

Left: *The main entrance to Kensal Green Cemetery.*

Below: *The plain and business-like memorial on the Brunel family plot which is just a stone's throw from Isambard Kingdom Brunel's Great Western Railway lines.*

A painted advertisement for the London Co-operative Society, which had been hidden since the 1960s, revealed when the more modern advertising hoarding was removed in October 2005.

The brass balls of the restored pawnbroker's sign in Portobello Road.

Within the area we can also find hospitals that stand out with Victorian splendour. It is just a pity that Victorian splendour doesn't help the healing process and so modern functionality has had to take precedence. Although outside the borough, Du Cane Road Hospital is a prime example of an elegant building. It is a red-brick building with the green top dome that stands out like a beacon. The hospital's proper name is the Hammersmith Hospital and is a world-renowned centre of excellence; it is also where I was born in June 1954. It has the dubious privilege of also being located next door to Wormwood Scrubs Prison. The prison's gates are probably the most famous gates in the country and are easily recognisable.

The Princess Louise Hospital is another of the older medical establishments in the area, although its current building only dates from 1924 when it was erected by the people of Kensington for sick children. It was a striking building with iron railings around the outside, but unfortunately much of the original building has now gone to make way for the modern buildings needed for an efficient modern hospital.

Entertainment has always been an important part of community life and cinemas have played an important role. There were a number of cinemas in the area, however, not many have survived the changes in fashion. Firstly, some became bingo halls, then, as home entertainment took over, the cinemas just failed to make money and closed. As a child I would go to Saturday morning pictures at one of the two cinemas in Westbourne Grove. The ABC (Queens as we knew it, because it was adjacent to Queensway) or The Odeon (Oscar Deutz Entertains Our Nation) were both cinemas in the classic style, with the Odeon decorated in the company's typical house style of the 1950s. The ABC is now a restaurant but has maintained its typical ABC corporate façade. On Ladbroke Grove was another huge cinema which I think was the Royalty. It was on the corner of Lancaster Road and was built in typical red brick – very square and architecturally simple it was nevertheless an impressive establishment. The interior was decorated in the typical picture-palace style with lots of alabaster plaster fancy work painted in drab colours with gold detailing. The cinema closed in the 1960s but was used for a time as a bingo hall. It also had a particularly infamous member of staff who went on to meet his fate on the hangman's gallows. Christie, the notorious resident of 10 Rillington Place, is detailed elsewhere in this book.

The beautiful façade of Hammersmith Hospital in Du Cane Road.

Above left: *The Electric Cinema Portobello Road, one of the very first purpose-built film theatres in England.*

Above: *The ornate interior of the Electric Cinema.*

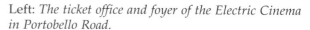

Left: *The ticket office and foyer of the Electric Cinema in Portobello Road.*

Notting Hill Gate and the Coronet in 2005.

Surprisingly one cinema that has survived is the Electric in Portobello Road. It is a smallish establishment (600 seats) that, during the flower-power 1960s, would show specialist films. It was always known by the young of the area as 'the flea pit' or 'bug hole', but it has kept up with the times and is still a going concern. The façade of the Electric is simple but it still seems to stand out amongst the other buildings adjacent to it. It was opened in February 1910 and was amongst the first cinemas built specifically as a film theatre. The building was designed by Gerald Seymour Valentin and still boasts a fabulous ornate plaster interior, even though it has been completely refurbished. In 1932 it was renamed The Imperial Playhouse – a name that lasted until it closed in 1970. Thankfully this wonderful little theatre reopened with a new name: Electric Cinema Club.

There is another cinema that is holding up a banner for the old-style independent cinemas of the early 1900s. This is a cinema that is even smaller than the Electric. The Gate in Notting Hill Gate was opened in 1911, although the building itself dates back to 1861. The original building was a restaurant called Harvey's Dining Room, but later its name was changed to the Golden Bells Coffee Palace and Restaurant. As a sideline the upper floor was operated as a brothel. It was the downstairs portion that was converted into a 450-seat cinema, named the Electric Palace, in April 1911.

Over the years the name has been changed to the Embassy in the early 1930s, and later to the Classic. It had an ornate domed entrance and façade that was lost during the bombing of London in the Second World War. However, it is fortunate that the interior has survived with its alabaster plaster and friendly comfortable atmosphere. Again it is still in business

and it too has undergone a full refurbishment.

As a bit of a novelty I felt we should include the most unusual listed building in the country. However it is just outside the area I had intended to write about, but it was such a memorable part of my childhood that I really wanted to include it. This listed building is actually the 'Elfin Oak' in Kensington Gardens, which of course is not a building and I am not even sure you can even call it architecture. The oak came originally from Richmond Park and was carved with small furry animals and elves by children's illustrator Ivor Innes. The oak is located at Black Lion Gate, Kensington Gardens and is well worth a visit.

Modern architecture is also well represented in the area with office blocks and high-rise flats dotted around the borough. One highly visible edifice can be seen from all over the area – the Trellick Tower in Golborne Road. But Trellick Tower is no ordinary block of flats. It was designed by Erno Goldfinger as his final commission but it was not received as well as he would have wanted. It became a high-rise centre for crime and antisocial behaviour. The building work started in 1968 and lasted four years. It was a solution to the requirement for affordable housing during the height of North Kensington's slum clearance and Westway period. The building stands 322 feet high, which equates to 31 storeys. It has 219 flats, all with large balconies and natural light from large expanses of glass. The flats are managed by a Tenants' Management Organisation (TMO) with only a small number being in private ownership. The flats rarely come onto the market, but their value in 2005 was between £150,000 and £200,000. Under the control of the TMO the reputation of the tower has changed – the stories of harassment by drug addicts and women

The Elfin Oak in Kensington Gardens.

Some of the Elfin folk climbing the Elfin Oak.

Above: *The Mother Black Cap pub being towered over by Erno Goldfinger's monolith Trellick Tower.*

Right: *The new skyline of Norland Road. Satellite dishes sprout like thorns from the side of the Norland towers.*

Below: *The new Frestonia office block.*

being assaulted within its confines have gone, and there is a concierge, security system and CCTV which has changed the tower from high-rise wasteland in to high-rise housing icon. The perception of the building has changed so much over the years that in 1998 the building was given a Grade II listing. This building was designed with a service tower to one side, containing the boiler house, lifts, stairs and rubbish chutes. The service tower is joined to the main structure every three floors which means that the flats on certain floors have the bedrooms lower than the entrance level – this is seen as chic in some circles.

Erno Goldfinger died in 1987, having retired some ten years earlier, but his tower stands as probably the last high-rise housing block to be built in this part of the UK. Its dominance of the North Kensington skyline will ensure that his work will be visible for many years to come.

Other high-rise developments in the area include those on Freston Road and Norland Road, parts of the Potteries and Piggeries of Notting Dale that in years gone by were famous for their poor housing and poverty. The new architecture was again conceived in the late 1960s when slum clearance was at its zenith and modernist architecture

was *de rigueur*. It is fortunate that, along with the modern design, the powers that be also chose to renovate and rebuild many of the older buildings which now stand side by side with their more modern counterparts.

It is not only housing that has sprung up in Notting Hill – industrial and office accommodation has also arrived but, as with the housing, they are in many cases well designed and modern or sympathetic refurbishments of older buildings. One complex has also revived a name that was synonymous with the struggle for good-quality affordable housing – Frestonia, a name that was chosen by squatters for a free and independent state in Freston Road has been adopted by the latest office complex being built in the borough, and it is just a stone's throw from the home of the original Frestonians. The beauty of any architecture is in the eye of the beholder and those that use or dwell in the buildings are the final judges – it is not for me to say what is good or important. I could say what I like or dislike but I am sure that as years pass these opinions will undoubtedly change. I wonder if the local residents of years gone by liked some of the modern and radical buildings of those times.

The Hackney-carriage drivers' hut at the junction of Kensington Park Road and Ladbroke Road, which goes back more than 120 years to a more genteel time when cabs were pulled by horses.

This lovely little house in the Addison Avenue part of Norland Town is nestled away near the corner of St James Square.

All Saints Church with its recognisable tower.

The tower of All Saints Church.

Left: *Some of the dedicated members of the congregation, including Victor Fergus and his wife.*

Below: *The interior of All Saints Church, viewed from the Clydesdale Road entrance.*

Chapter 3

Churches, Chapels, Convents
and Other Places of Worship

The religious buildings of the area are varied and splendid, and they certainly reflect the diversity of the residents. Almost from day one the skyline has contained the towers and spires of churches. On the lanes and streets of Victorian Notting Hill these magnificent structures stood out as masterpieces of architectural excellence.

Probably the most recognisable church in the area is All Saints Church, located on Talbot Road. I have to confess a personal love for All Saints, mainly because it was, or should I say its grounds were, my playground as a child. Looking back it was a little irreverent, but as children we would explore anywhere we were not supposed to. Behind the church was the living accommodation for a number of the clergy, and we never knew how but they always seemed to know when we were playing in the grounds and would come to chase us off. The church had a hall attached which was used for wedding receptions and other events. But for us kids the highlight was the bands that used to practice there. Some of the bands would allow us to sit in and watch. Among those that came to All Saints Hall to practice was Chris Sandford, who at the time was in 'Coronation Street' and had a hit record called 'Not too little, Not too much', which spent nine weeks in the charts at the end of 1963, peaking at number 17.

Early in 1965 a gentleman from the valleys of Wales came to the hall, having already entered the charts. That gentleman was Tom Jones, mind you, he didn't have to walk far as at the time he had a flat in

Clydesdale Road. As soon as the news spread of who was practising the females of the area descended on the place like a swarm. My sister still has his autograph on an old slip of paper.

Getting back to the church itself, the tower is very recognisable and can be seen from all over the neighbourhood. It is a very robust and business-like tower, and certainly stands out when you are travelling along the Westway extension or looking out for it from the tube train between Ladbroke Grove and Westbourne Park. Had its founder and benefactor, Revd Dr Walker, fulfilled his wishes the church would have been topped with an even more substantial spire. The dream of Dr Walker was to cap the tower with a 100-foot spire 'as lofty as that of Salisbury Cathedral', and had it come to fruition it would certainly have been the most impressive spire in England. Originally the church was dedicated to St Ann but it was soon renamed All Saints, even though it was known locally as 'All Sinners in the Mud' or 'Walkers Folly'. The name 'All Sinners in the Mud' is a reference to the fact that it was surrounded by fields with a pond and open ground that was frequented by gypsies. All Saints Church was erected in memory of Dr Walker's parents and was to be the centrepiece of a 'new town', which was never completed but swallowed up by the rest of Notting Hill. The interior of the church is fairly plain with English marble columns. However, it is a grand space and when entering from the Clydesdale Road entrance you are immediately drawn into the atmosphere. It is a welcoming space with the stained-glass window and altar at the opposite end to the entrance. I looked in the church on a recent walk around the area and found the welcoming hand of Sam Johnson-Paul at the door, inviting me in for the Sunday service. The congregation was in good voice and made full use of the superb acoustics in the main body of the church. I was pleased to see a good cross-section of the community at worship – young and old, black and white and everything in between, a welcoming and harmonious sight indeed.

One thing that has changed since my youth is the fact that Talbot Road between Clydesdale Road and Powis Gardens is now closed to traffic, which makes the church seem calmer and even more regal, but by the same token closer to the passerby. Trees grow all around the church and the large crucifix still stands in the small corner garden at the Clydesdale Road end of the church. At Christmas a nativity scene was set up in this area to cheer the passing members of

Victor Fergus fund-raising outside All Saints Church.

41

the public. The main structure of the church was completed in 1855 but it was some years before windows and furniture were added. The church was finally consecrated on 9 April 1861 and has been in use almost constantly since that date – there was a break in its use during the Second World War.

The church was damaged by enemy action on 26 September 1940, which rendered the church unusable. In March 1944 the vicarage was burnt down and also became unusable, which meant that the community was faced with having no place of worship. Temporary repairs were carried out to the church in April 1944, but this turned out to be short-lived as the Luftwaffe succeeded in closing the church for a second time in June 1944, when it was again seriously damaged. The closure of the church on this occasion meant that the services had to be held elsewhere. So for this period St Columbs in Lancaster Road was used by the congregation. The church was finally reopened, having been fully refurbished, in April 1951 – six years after the end of the war.

It is only polite to acknowledge the sources of information included in this book, so to that end I thank All Saints Church. Please visit the church and enter by the Clydesdale Road entrance. Just inside the door on the left-hand wall is a plaque giving all the significant dates associated with the church, but don't just turn and leave – turn right and take a look through the glass-panelled inner doors – I promise it will be worth it.

Well that's the building, but a church needs its congregation and helpers, so on a Saturday morning in August 2005 I went along to All Saints Church and met some members of the congregation. Victor Fergus and his wife were outside the Clydesdale Road entrance setting up a stall as part of a fund-raising and church-awareness initiative. Victor took time out to have a chat inside the church and told me:

I have been in the UK since 1960 when I came from the Caribbean to join my parents who had been here since the early '50s – they came here with the first wave of West Indian immigrants and settled in Notting Hill where they joined the community here at All Saints Church. When I came here I think they had already been through the problem years, but even saying that I have seen changes in the area. I have been coming to All Saints Church from my first days in England because, as I said, it was already my parents' church. We have seen all the phases that a community goes through. Clearly it was difficult at first, but we have a wonderfully loving, honest and friendly community. The area itself is now going through a phase of gentrification, but we've seen it all before and in the end it just goes full circle, back to the warm and friendly community we all love. This is an area and a church where new immigrants come – people say 'do we mix?' – well you have no choice, you have to mix. It is illustrated when the congregation has a get-together and we all bring in food. We all know who

brought what food, and even though it's from all parts of the world, its like one big melting-pot. We have seen many different nationalities come into the community over the years and at the moment it is Eastern Europeans, and I would say they are also now integrating absolutely brilliantly both into the area and into the church community – it's as if they've always been here and the church is like a second home.

Victor went on to speak of his life in the community:

I went to Bevington Road School as a small child and then on to Isaac Newton School in Lancaster Road. All through those years at school I have served in the Church, but as a small child I didn't like it. In earlier years the church meant something to the school and they encouraged us, but it was hard because once a week I had to be the server, so at six o'clock in the morning I had to come here to the church. I'd do my serving duty and then go to school. It was a time when the headmasters were proud of their links with the church and they would point out to the other pupils that you were a server at your church – of course as a young boy I would cringe at this. One of my memories of those early years was being somewhat irreverent towards the vicarage – as a child I would never walk down the stairs but slide down the banister. Now that was good fun.

I am a father myself now and have a son and a daughter. My son is now a server, so that's three generations of my family that have worshipped here at All Saints Church.

I asked Victor about the carnival, its position and impact on the church, and of course if he thought the troubles of a few years ago had bonded the community together:

I think that people read that carnival trouble completely wrong – you see the same sort of thing happened in Birmingham, Manchester and Bristol etc., so it wasn't just a community thing. It was something in society that was boiling for a long time and it had to come out – unfortunately for us it came out at the carnival. So to answer your original question, now the issues that caused the problems in various communities have been addressed, as a result of the trouble, yes it has bonded our community. I always say to people 'come down to All Saints Church during one of the carnival days', because this church is open and we get people coming in, breaking off from their dancing and enjoyment to pray. Sometimes we have to laugh because they come in and then stop and realise they have a can of beer in their hand, so they back out slowly, leave their drink outside then come back in to the church. Sam Johnson-Paul who has been at the church for many many years, has some stories of people that come into All Saints to pray year after year – they are obviously from other churches or even from other areas, because that's the only time we see them.

You know the church is now right up with modern technology. [In 2006] we have our own website at www.allsaintsnottinghill.org.uk, which is packed with pictures and information.

Just a stone's throw from All Saints Church is a chapel of very different style. With the gardens carefully restored and kept neat, the Romanesque façade of the Talbot Tabernacle stands out, proudly facing Talbot Road. The red-brick edifice was built in 1888 under the watchful eye of the then pastor Frank Henry White. Mr White was well respected and loved as a pastor, and he was the incumbent for 30 years between 1876 and 1906. The current building was erected to replace the old tin chapel as a non-sectarian Church of Christ, which had been erected in 1869. Prior to this services had been held in the Victoria Hall in Archer Street for two years by Gordon Furlong. It was Mr Furlong that had raised the funds and organised the building of the old iron chapel. At the time of writing the Talbot Tabernacle has a new and exciting use as the Tabernacle Arts Centre.

The Talbot Tabernacle was very influential in Maureen Marshall's life. Maureen was then known as Maureen Wilkinson and was, and is, my sister. For a long time she was a member of the Talbot Tabernacle Sunday School and, indeed, various clubs and groups run by the Tabernacle. Maureen takes up her story:

My first memories of Talbot Tabernacle are in the early '60s, when I attended Sunday school there on a Sunday afternoon. At the time the Tabernacle seemed an enormous building, with several back rooms as well as the large main church. Sunday school was in various rooms at the back of the Tabernacle, depending on the age of the children. Very often on a Sunday myself and a friend would stay after Sunday school for tea and then go on to the evening service.

Learning about the Scriptures was very important – it was not just learnt parrot fashion, but as an exciting and interesting story. I remember learning about the journeys of Saint Paul and taking a test set by the Scripture Union. I still have the Bible which was my prize – it was a very proud moment when it was presented to me during the Sunday service.

Sunday school was just a small part of church life, there were other clubs and meetings on weekday evenings, Junior Christian Endeavour, Ambassadors and missionary fellowship to name just three. On Missionary Fellowship evenings we would make toys such as skittles from empty cotton reels and scrapbooks. These were then sent overseas to children in very poor countries.

During the school holidays there would be activities run by The London City Mission. These were held in the grounds if the weather was fine or inside on wet days. Looking back, the Tabernacle was very much part of the community.

The highlight of the year was the summer outing – the one I remember the most was to Burnham Beeches which seemed to be right in the heart of the countryside. Although it was only a few miles outside London it was a world away from the inner city in which I lived. On another occasion we were taken to Woodford to visit one of the ministers who had moved to the area. We had a visit to a local park for games and then back to the minister's house for tea in the back garden. Unfortunately I can't remember his name, as this was over 40 years ago. I can, however, remember Miss Starsmere, one of the very dedicated Sunday-school teachers who gave up their time to the children in the area.

Looking back, the Tabernacle, although a very impressive building, was secondary to the very kind and dedicated people who made up the church. This was a very happy time of my life and one I will never forget.

At the top end of Ladbroke Grove stands the Church of St John the Evangelist, a fine building designed by Messrs Stevens and Alexander and built by Mr Hicks. The church was designed to house 1,500 worshippers. It was consecrated on 29 January 1845 with its first incumbent being Revd William Holdsworth. It is again a magnificent church that had been known as St John's in the Hayfields because of its rural location. It is located some 100 feet above sea level and in its early days the church would have been seen standing on top of the St John's Hill by the poor of Notting Dale. However, it was seen as a church for the 'snobs and upper classes' – this was a factor that led to the Anglican Church setting up in Lancaster Road, to give

St Peter's Church, Kensington Park Road. Its style gives it the look of a typical Italian basilica.

Above: *The Romanesque front elevation of the Talbot Tabernacle, which is now used as an arts centre.*

Below: *The former Congregational Chapel in Lancaster Road is used as a recording studio in 2006.*

Above: *St John the Evangelist Church, which was known as St John's in the Hayfields.*

Below: *The Roman Catholic Church of St Mary of the Angels in Westmorland Road.*

St Peter's, seen from Portobello Road.

The Westbourne Grove Baptist Chapel.

the poor somewhere to worship – a move that led to sufficient funds being raised to build the Church of St Clement's.

The Church of St John in 2006 sits in St John Gardens and Lonsdale Crescent and is surrounded by grass and trees. There are substantial villas on all four sides but the church is still as prominent. It is a stone structure with tall spire which almost glows white in the sunshine – it must have made a beautiful sight in the days when it was seen from miles away, and by the same token affording a magnificent view from its spire down the Thames Valley as far as Windsor and beyond.

The religious buildings of Notting Hill are not only limited to the large typically English style but are designed in many different and interesting styles. By walking around the streets we can find Grecian, Romanesque, Italian and styles from all periods but somehow they all fit in seamlessly. We can find both large and small, some with fascinating histories and stories.

The architecture of the religious buildings in Notting Hill is varied and splendid, and we shall illustrate this with a look at an Italianate design in Kensington Park Road. St Peter's is a fabulous church which was designed by Thomas Allom and consecrated in 1857. Its tower gives the skyline above the Portobello Road antique shops a surreal aspect. It is in perfect proportion with the large buildings around it, and when looking at it from Portobello Road it doesn't seem to dominate the smaller buildings it

looks over. It is a fact that in the Victorian London sickness was rarely minor and to prove this point there is a memorial within the church dedicated to the wife of its first rector, Revd F.H. Addams. Mrs Addams died whilst nursing her five children through scarlet fever, a consequence of Victorian ignorance of the spread of infectious diseases.

It is difficult to say where the style of the old Congregational Chapel originates from, but as a child I thought it looked Greek or Roman and the business that had taken the premises over did much to perpetuate these thoughts. In the 1960s a resin or fibreglass company that made imitation stone ornaments and statues occupied the building. The goods were left outside to dry and they really set off the style of the chapel.

The chapel's foundation-stone was laid in 1865, which would indicate, by looking at old maps, that this building also stood rather grandly and a little lonely in open fields. Its first incumbent was Revd James Russell, who by all accounts was a particularly good minister and took his position very seriously. In later years, as previously mentioned, the chapel was used as business premises. The only record of the chapel's commercial use is of the imitation stoneware manufacturers. However, when that business moved on it was to be the first step in a new and somewhat famous chapter in the history of this fine building. The Congregational Chapel stands on the corner of Lancaster Road and Basin Street and in 2006 is a recording studio owned by the Trevor Horne

45

Right: *The Elgin public house, which stands opposite the former site of the Franciscan convent that was founded by Cardinal Manning.*

Below inset: *The Franciscan convent in Portobello Road, now used as the Spanish School.*

Bottom: *Ladbroke Grove in the 1920s. The high walls of the now demolished Franciscan convent are just visible.*

Organisation. In its first foray into the music business it was the home of Chris Blackwell's Island Record Company, and indeed its home through its most important years. Many great artists have recorded in the chapel's studios, but it is the Band Aid records that are its most enduring legacy.

And of the Roman Catholic community? There is another fine English church dedicated to St Mary of the Angels located in Westmorland Road. It is one of the most sturdy looking buildings in the area. The church was built in the 1850s and has been served by both Cardinal Wiseman and Cardinal Manning.

The Westbourne Grove Baptist Chapel located on the junction of Ledbury Road and Westbourne Grove (formerly Norfolk Terrace) was built in 1856 with funds raised by the congregation of the overcrowded chapel in Silver Street, in the village of Kensington Gravel Pits. The influence behind the building project was Revd W.G. Lewis who, having made a success of the Silver Street chapel, went on to attract large and regular congregations to the new building. Unfortunately the building is no longer a place of worship but it has been saved and still stands proud with its pair of octagonal towers and main body now cleaned and renovated.

Having put pen to paper to describe the fine churches and chapels of Notting Hill and Dale we must not forget that there were also convents within the district, and so the best place to start with convents is on Portobello Road. The large Franciscan convent was built on the opposite side of the lane (Portobello Road) to Portobello Farm in 1862, only a few years before the farm was demolished. As well as the convent the sisters ran a home for children known as the St Elizabeth's Home on the same site. However, even in the world of convents things change and the building had new occupants by the late-eighteenth century. Although the distinctive building remained intact the convent was, from 1896, in the hands of a Dominican order and the children's home became the St Anne's Home for Working Girls and a school for children suffering from diseases of the eyes. Although the building has remained more or less unchanged, it now has a new set of residents.

The convent has become the Spanish School, an establishment that is detailed elsewhere in this book.

Although not strictly a convent, or even a house of worship, Portobello Farm and its land also became associated with an order of nuns. Opposite the then Franciscan convent the 'little sisters of the poor' obtained the farmhouse and 12 acres of land from the Talbot family. On this land they proceeded to build the 'St Josephs Home for the Aged' in 1866. The sisters belonged to the order of St Servan Brittany and as part of their service would move to different establishments on a five-year rota – even though most of the nuns were English the order only spoke in French. Life as a nun in this enclosed order was hard with only a few letters and two visits per year allowed, but with all the discipline the order was democratic and the sisters would take it in turns to be 'Mother Superior'. As for the building, it was a large austere building, built from dark-brown brick with four storeys plus loft rooms, and a bow-topped double door entrance on Portobello Road. The home was finally demolished in the 1970s and all that remains is part of the outside brick wall along Portobello Road.

Along Ladbroke Grove at the junction of Westbourne Park Road there used to be a convent, which has now completely gone. The Franciscan convent was founded in 1859 by the then Father (later to be Cardinal) Manning on low ground opposite a tavern known as the Lord Elgin on Ladbroke Grove. Withy beds clearly indicated the course of a stream which ran down from the Portobello Lane area and by the gardens of the convent. The convent occupied one and three quarter acres and housed about 30 nuns. It was surrounded by a particularly high all-encircling wall of a very sturdy nature. The walls were clearly designed to save the nuns from prying eyes, however this was before the No. 7 double-decker buses that passed within feet of the convent in later years. Both the convent and the old tavern have now gone, with flats occupying the site of the convent and a newer hostelry, The Elgin, replacing the old tavern and skittle alley.

As far as monasteries are concerned, the Carmelite community is represented in Exmoor

The synagogue in Kensington Park Road, now used by the Montessori School.

The Carmelite Monastery in Exmoor Street.

The façade of the Horbury Chapel.

St Michael's Church on Ladbroke Grove.

The Salvation Army hall in Portobello Road.

The Church of St Andrew's at the Great Western Road end of Tavistock Crescent.

St Stephen's Church at the top of Talbot Road.

Street and is located in what appears to be a sprawling set of buildings built in brick and topped with a typical set of slate roofs. The bricks are now brown and stained but it's former beauty is obvious.

The Jewish community in the area also had its place of worship, albeit not in the typical style of building you would expect of a synagogue. The synagogue is located at the Westbourne Park Road end of Kensington Park Road. The local Jewish community was located in and around the Kensington Park Road area with their own shops and many worshippers living in adjacent roads. The Montessori School now occupies the building.

Even having written about so many places of worship there are still more that should be mentioned – the Horbury Chapel and school was built in 1849, its façade is flanked by a pair of Norman-like towers, and it stands proud at the junction of Kensington Park Road and Ladbroke Road. It was here that the so-called 'Kensington parliament' met. The parliament was a debating society which attracted and developed a number of important and powerful public figures.

Then there is St Michael's Church in Faraday Road, as well s the Churches of St Charles, St Andrew and many more, some large, some small, some pretty and some not and indeed some that have survived and some that have not. Those that haven't survived include St Luke's which was destroyed by fire in

1969, a sad event that I witnessed as a child and, of course, Norland Castle, the Salvation Army Citadel.

In terms of other non-Christian places of worship we can also find in Norland Road the Central Gurdwara London Sikh Temple, with its golden dome and brilliant-white paint work, and in other parts of the borough such buildings as the Notting Hill Mosque. There are, of course, many places of worship for many different faiths in the area, where the members of the community can be found celebrating their beliefs in small and inconspicuous surroundings. This is exactly what makes this such a diverse and cosmopolitan community.

Norland Road with the Central Gurdwara London Sikh Temple in the background. It is on the former location of Norland Castle, the Salvation Army Citadel.

Above: *The interior of St Francis of Assisi Church on Pottery Lane.*

Left: *The pretty courtyard of St Francis of Assisi.*

Left: *The school building of St Francis. Note the roof-top play area.*

Below: *Latimer School in Freston Road.*

Chapter 4
Places of Learning – Street and School

It has to be said that, as a common London boy, much of my education was gained in the streets, parks and less salubrious areas of Notting Hill. However, that does not mean that I neither enjoyed nor am ungrateful for the education I received at the schools that I attended. Maybe it is that I am a firm believer in a balanced education and a preparation for the greater university that we call life. I attended one nursery/infants/primary school (Colville School) and one senior school (Sir Christopher Wren School in Shepherd's Bush), and from school went on to college in Croydon. Many may say that I was lucky to have had an education that didn't require me to move from one educational emporium to another, but I would add that I learnt some of the equally important and relevant life skills in Portobello Road Market, youth clubs and on the street corners of Notting Hill. It is for these reasons that I am writing this chapter – one that I have enjoyed researching as it has brought back many happy memories. To the London County Council (LCC) and Greater London Council (GLC) who ran the schools I attended, and the market people who augmented my education, I thank you – I turned out OK.

It would be easy to continue with a list of schools in the area but their quality and history demands that more meat is added to the bones of this chapter. Education in the area started with voluntary, ragged and Church schools in the early-nineteenth century with community clubs augmenting the education with pleasurable pastimes, sport, penny dinners and Sunday schooling. In the Potteries and Piggeries, clubs grew up that where sponsored by the nobility and wealthy of the day, establishments with names like Rugby, Latymer and Harrow Clubs.

An early establishment in Notting Dale was the Harrow School Mission run by Revd William Law, a post he took up following a curacy at St Mary Abbots in Kensington. I make no apology for copying down the following as it is both touching and poignant:

Nothing could have been more forlorn or desolate than the condition of this district at starting. The station of the metropolitan railway [now the Hammersmith and City] which bears the name Latimer Road was familiarly known as 'Piggery Junction' from the miserable and unwholesome establishment for the feeding of those animals which then occupied the site of our church and mission room. The livelihood of the men, brickmakers, costermongers, casual labourers, was always precarious, while the women, the real breadwinners of the family, where mainly employed in steam laundries, away from their homes and children. Rich inhabitants there were none: the moderately poor were scarce.

These are the words of Revd Law upon being appointed to run the Harrow School Mission.

The mission was set up in two rooms of inadequate dimensions in Bard Street, but Law was not a man to rest on his laurels and he had raised enough funds by 1884 to build a two-storey building on land in Latimer Road known as Oyster Shell Square, so-called because the plot was occupied by pigsties and discarded oyster shells. The first church was well utilised but just three years later brick-built premises replaced it.

Law was a man of high principles and believed that the mission should take an active role in ensuring the young were safe while their parents were away from home working or drinking in the pubs in

The Harrow Club in Freston Road.

The crest of the Harrow Club.

the evenings. He worked tirelessly to save the young from seeking 'warmth and comfort and luxury in the gin palaces' by creating 'working men's clubs and reading rooms'.

Prior to the Harrow Mission, instructions on Christian values and basic skills were obtained at the Latymer Road Mission (note the spelling) which was originally run as a 'Ragged School', located in Blechynden Street. However, later legislation for compulsory education meant that the Latymer Road Mission changed its function into an 'Evening Institute for Boys'. It was informal and encouraged the young to come in off the streets with simple Christian teaching, a gymnasium and a farthing bank (a farthing being a quarter of a penny). The weekend saw the 'cocoa concerts', when a penny entrance fee not only paid for entertainment but also a cup of cocoa and a cake.

By 1880 the mission was catering for the working mothers and introduced a nursery facility which allowed the 'laundry women' to carry on their trade while their offspring were well cared for. The laundry women would take in washing from more well-off parts of the area and would work long, hard hours – the crèche was a godsend and opened from 7.30am until 9pm, with the assurance of the children being well fed and looked after in satisfactory conditions.

The third of the missions in the area, like the Harrow Mission, was run with links to a well-established public school. This club was the Rugby Home Mission. In 1889, following a short period in Wilsham Street, land was acquired in Walmer Road and, with support from Rugby School, club premises were established in the old bus yard. The original reason for setting up the boys' club lies with the fiancé of the club's founder, Arthur Walrond, who was involved in running a girls' club in St Anns Road that had suffered the age-old problem of the attention of young local boys. The boys would interrupt the girls' lessons and activities by throwing mud at the windows and generally being unruly, to such an extent that Arthur Walrond was asked to police the perimeter of the St Anns Road club. His lack of success led him to the conclusion that a similar establishment for the boys in a different location might be more successful. The new premises in Walmer Road were well equipped, having, of all things, a swimming-pool, which was possibly one of the earliest private pools in London. The club became incredibly successful and in spite of its tough reputation many famous explorers and scientists visited to give talks and shows to the boys. The boxing club produced many champions with the likes of Kipper Allum, Arthur Goom and Alf Mancini, as well as Lonsdale belt-holder Digger Stanley.

The older pupils of Rugby School were encouraged to help the poor of the Dale by teaching swimming and cricket, which was beneficial to all.

Up to this point all I have written about the Rugby Club was in the past tense – however that will now change. The Rugby Club is still alive and operating in Notting Dale, although the original building has been demolished. It means that this fine establishment has been in constant operation for well over 100 years. The club in Walmer Road and a sister club known as the Bradby Club for young people, which is located in Rugby, still meet for the annual cricket match with the Rugby School pupils and staff at the school's south coast sports facility. The 'mums' from Notting Dale also visit Rugby School annually – a tradition that has lasted in excess of 50 years.

In the London club boxing continues and competitions are regular events, with tournaments such as the Grand Open Boxing Championship being held to raise money for the 'Dale Youth ABC'. The Harrow Club is also alive and kicking, and is located in Freston Road – it claims a fine pedigree in the footballing arena with Les Ferdinand MBE, former England and Queens Park Rangers star, amongst its old boys.

The Latymer Club name also carries on with Latimer Road School located opposite the Harrow Club in Freston Road.

The Roman Catholic community of the area, which consisted mainly of Irish migrants and gypsies, sought a religious base for their education which would be an extension to the usual Sunday worship. The St Francis of Assisi Church and School was founded in 1860 in the poorest part of Notting Dale. Its first incumbent was Father Henry Rawes, a man who had been an Anglican clergyman but converted to the Catholic faith at the time of the Oxford movement.

The church and school were located in Pottery Lane and were squeezed in amongst stables and a pub, just a stone's throw from the bottle kilns of the potteries. The church attracted a good number of attendees, as did the school, but the congregation was always dependant upon the availability of suitable clean clothing and the onset of sobriety. Those attending were the poorest of the area with the women being laundry workers who had little time for their

Notting Dale hero and Rugby Mission boxer Alf Mancini during the mid-1920s.

The Wesleyan Chapel on Lancaster Road.

St Peter's Church School on Portobello Road.

offspring's need for suitable clothes for school and church. By the same token the adults found it hard to get the balance between church and pub correct. However, the St Francis of Assisi School and Church were still a success with more than adequate levels of attendance.

It was not only the Catholic community that could boast a church-affiliated school – the Anglican Church also understood the need for schooling and Sunday worship, and to this end also established premises in the area. At first the church was no more than a tin shack located at the opposite end of Walmer Road to the church of St Francis, on the corner of Lancaster Road. Revd Arthur Delgarno Robinson set his mind to fund-raising and by 1866, with many generous donations and gifts, the church and school of St Clement's was built. It is said that the steeple was built particularly low in order to not be too imposing, and that its clock became the time-piece of the community.

The site of the old tin church that had been used by the Anglicans was also used at a later date by the Methodists, prior to the construction of a fine new building on the corner of Silchester Road and Lancaster Road. The new and impressive Wesleyan Methodist chapel was completed in 1880. The Methodists had run the first Sunday school in the area and by 1882 it had grown to the point that it had 600 children on its register and required 24 staff to run it. But it wasn't just a Sunday school – the church also provided visiting campaigns and distributed tracts. It was its declared

aim to become 'a powerful agent for good in the area' – this was to be quite a task for, as with the other missions and churches in the Potteries, they had come to not only the poorest part of Notting Dale but what was probably the poorest part of London.

Outside the Potteries and Piggeries other schools were providing education to a slightly better-off community – this education, of course, needed paying for. Many children at this time would work in order to supplement meagre incomes and very often education was not a priority, but there was still enough to make schools like St Peter's a success. The school was built in 1862 with money raised by private subscription, church collections and a government grant amounting to the sum of £330. The school provided education for 96 boys and a similar number of girls, each of whom would pay a few pence a week in exchange for a basic education.

The school's success and rising population meant that in later years the elementary school register would consist of some 300 pupils and an infants' school of a further 200 younger children.

By the late 1860s education in London was coming of age and the church and missionary schools that had given such an admirable service to the young of the area with their limited funds and voluntary help were becoming overstretched. What was needed were regular and state-run schools. Better health care and increased awareness of hygiene meant that there was a great improvement in the infant mortality rate, which led to an ever-increasing number of young in the community.

By 1870 Parliament was to initiate the start of state education and as a first move implemented the Education Act, which allowed local authorities to raise funds from local rates to provide school places for every child. The area of Notting Dale and Kensington was controlled by the School Board for London which, in its early years, built the Portobello School on Portobello Road, which opened in 1876. The school catered for both boys and girls and was considered at the time to be 'a very good educational establishment'. The new education system allowed separate classes for different age groups – something that until this era was difficult and probably seen as unnecessary. The school provided for infants in mixed-sex classes – thereafter the sexes were taught separately throughout the school, until the children left aged 13. The school was large and airy with outdoor playgrounds and well-equipped classrooms. There were separate entrances for boys and girls, something that was a standard feature of schools of the time, and above the gates was the carved head-stone with the cipher of the London School Board. In the late 1940s education underwent some major changes – the leaving age was raised to 15, which meant that the volume of pupils was increased so schools were separated into infant/junior schools and senior schools. As a result infant/junior schools took pupils up to age 11 and senior schools to at least 15. The changes meant that the Portobello School became the North Kensington Mixed School, a name that would only last a few years as it soon became Isaac Newton School, a secondary school for boys. The girls of the area got their education at Ladbroke School. Again this was to be a relatively short-lived situation. Slum clearances in the area led to a falling school population and both Isaac Newton and Ladbroke were closed by the mid-1970s. Pupils found themselves travelling to the eastern end of the borough to attend Holland Park Comprehensive School.

Of the old school buildings, Portobello School is now used as a professional development centre for Kensington and Chelsea teachers. The gates in Portobello Road can still be seen near the railway bridge, and I am glad to say that the old school buildings still remain mostly unchanged. Ladbroke School is now the Lighthouse Centre (a support centre run by the Terrence Higgins Trust), but again still looks almost as it did during its years as a school.

Within three years of the Portobello

The name plaque of Buckingham Terrace School, which later became Colville Junior School.

School being opened a second school started taking pupils. It is this school that I have a personal knowledge of – the school was originally called Buckingham Terrace School but in later years changed its name to Colville Junior Mixed. It took pupils from the surrounding area, many of whom had been pupils at the Colville Mews ragged school. It was built in a similar style and with similar rules and standards as Portobello School and again under the control of the School Board of London.

I attended Colville School from about three years old, in the nursery, until I was 11 when I left to attend Christopher Wren School in Shepherd's Bush. I was embarrassed to realise, whilst looking around the outside recently, that during those years as a pupil I had never noticed either the 'S.B.' of 'L.' cipher, or the name

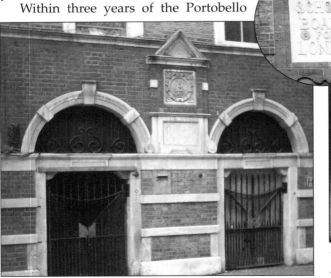

The gates of Portobello School and (inset) cipher of the School Board of London.

The twin entrances and staircases of Colville Junior School – girls to the left, boys to the right and infants in the centre. The boys' and girls' entrances and staircases are built parallel and lead to exactly the same places.

The Lancaster Road entrance to the Isaac Newton Development Centre, formerly Isaac Newton School and originally the Portobello School.

The laundry block in the boys' playground of Colville School. In 2006 the building is used as a music room, but was used for art classes in the 1960s.

'Buckingham Terrace School' on its wall. What I had seen was the carvings over the gates that read 'Boys Entrance' and 'Girls Entrance', although when I attended the practice of separating the sexes had long since died out.

Buckingham Terrace School opened on 7 June 1879 and provided 587 places for the local children. These places had to be paid for and a fee of two pence per day was levied on each pupil. The pupils would attend classes in the tiered classrooms, each tier being for children of different academic abilities, with some classes being as large as 60. Holidays were short and the regime strict, and even the teachers had to toe the line. The Colville School parent-teacher's association put together a book to celebrate 125 years of the school and within the publication listed some of the rules – and I should point out these were for the teachers not the pupils.

Female Teachers
No bloomers, no showing of ankles
No ten inch bustle extensions
No joining feminist movements
No marriage or other unseemly behaviour

Male Teachers
No rolled or unlinked shirt sleeves
No closely cropped hair

Male and Female Teachers
No smoking, no drinking
No visiting dance or billiard halls

Teachers were also expected to clean the classrooms with soap once a week, wash the windows and check the outhouses daily (up until 1889 the school did not have flush toilets but simple troughs that needed

emptying by hand). Discipline was such that the cane was the standard punishment for even minor misdemeanours.

In its original form only the centre part of the buildings existed but by 1884 (only five years after opening) demand was such that one wing was added which increased the capacity by 600, but it wasn't long before the school was once again becoming too overcrowded. In 1906 the School Board decided to buy extra land to again increase the school capacity, but it was not until 1913 that work was completed on the third wing of the main building.

The name of the school changed to Colville School in 1939 and by 1948 it had split into two separate schools – Colville Junior Mixed and Colville Infants School, but it once again amalgamated to form Colville Primary School in 1976.

During the First World War the school carried on as normal, although with many of the local men away at the Front, woman and even children staffed the factories and towards the end of hostilities rationing meant that food was scarce. During the Second World War the ground floor was used as a fire station and, with bombs falling all around during the Blitz, many pupils were evacuated, leaving London from Paddington Station to stay with families in the country. The blocks of flats opposite Colville School (Portobello Court) are the result of combined efforts of the Luftwaffe's bombing and slum clearance.

After the war the school started to get back to normal. However, it was a mess – not as a result of direct hits by German bombs, but because of its secondary use as a fire-service base and collateral damage from near misses.

The headmistress, Miss Hirons (who was still there when I attended the school), wrote of the conditions she, her staff and pupils had to cope with even in 1949 when she was appointed:

Much of the building was derelict and unusable. The rooms were piled high with debris and the floors torn up

The Colville School class of 1958. Left to right, back row: *Jennifer Barnstable, Bobby Barrance, Geraldine ?, Pauline Piper, ?, ?, Angela ?, ?;* middle row: *?, Barbara Fry, Shirley Hearon, Brenda Carr, Jennifer Sollis, Linda Shepard, ?, Sally Cox;* front row: *Marrion Willams, ?, Susan Keen.*

and broken. *The whole building was dismal and run down... There were still 48 coal-fires in the building.*

Tony Rawlings attended Colville and has particular memories of the playground and the dining-room:

As I remember it the dining-room was at the front of the school building and just below the level of the street, so you could look out the windows and see the legs of people passing by. The boys' playground was at the Portobello Road end – over to the right was a covered area with benches and, where the entrance gate was located, steps led down, which was good because there could be two games of cricket going on at the same time, one either side of the steps. I saw that film Notting Hill *and the shop Hugh Grant ran was in Portobello Road – in one scene you could see between the shops to the school. But it has changed – when I was a pupil the big gate wasn't there, I think it was a brick wall.*

There was [sic] some tough kids at that school then, bearing in mind they only went up to 11 years. I remember one boy, I can't remember his name now, but he'd been getting hassle from this other kid, so the next day come the end of school he chased him down the road with a cut-throat razor – good job me and some other boys stopped him or who knows what would have happened.

I remember when it came time for the 11-plus [the final exam of junior school – the grade you got dictated what school you could go to], the day before, I had to take a note home telling my parents I needn't attend. I went through much of my life thinking I was stupid until many years later when I was diagnosed with dyslexia – of course that was unheard of when I was a kid – they just branded me stupid.

Of all the pupils that Colville has produced, the school and community are rightly proud of one who is probably its most famous – Daley Thompson was at the school at the same time as I was. However, our paths never crossed as he is a few years younger than I am, which is my regret as he is a hero of mine. He was born in 1958 in Notting Hill to Scottish and Nigerian parents and at age 18 competed in his first Olympics in Montreal, where he achieved a finishing position of eighteenth. Four years later in 1980 he was to take top honours in Moscow and in doing so made the decathlon one of the most popular events in the Olympics.

Daley won his second Olympic gold medal for the decathlon in 1984 making him only the second athlete in the history of the Olympics to do so. The decathlon consists of ten events including three throwing disciplines, four running, two jumping and the pole vault, all of which makes the winner the all-round athletic champion. Daley went on to be recognised for his services to athletics by receiving an MBE in 1982 which was elevated to a CBE in 2000, and he was also voted Sports Personality of the Year in 1982. All in all, this great sportsman is a fine example to all those that enjoy and participate in sports.

I had the very great pleasure of being invited to Colville during my research, and I have to say I was stunned by the emotions I felt as I stood in the playground for the first time in 40 years – I was absolutely speechless. I remembered how I felt on my first day at school and how big the whole place seemed. The building is listed and protected against changes – this is a blessing because, apart from the new nursery building erected in the playground and the outside

Above: *Teaching in 1951 at Colville School. Note the tiered rows of desks.*

Right: *Prize giving at Colville School in 1958. Receiving her prize is Delia Guiltenane. Others waiting to collect their prizes are, left to right: Ian ?, Steven ?, Lenni Hyatt, Janet Hogan, Stewart Hatton. Miss Hirons is at the head of the queue with her list of prizewinners.*

Prize day in 1958. The photograph includes: Delia Guiltenane, Julie Dike, Helen ?, Susan Brown, Marion Joseph, Stephanie Batten, Janet Hogan, Linda Smith, Ann Wise, Christine Glover, Shirley Smith, Beatrice ?, Charles ?, Barry Dunsford. The children had been dancing for the parents and VIPs – a performance which was also given at Kensington Town Hall.

The Colville School nativity play in the early 1960s. Unfortunately the only name I know is my own, and I am on the right of the front row.

Above: *A school production of* The Pied Piper of Hamelin *in 1958. The 'town councillors' (seated) are Jennifer Sollis, Bobby Barrance (with glasses) and Roger Fletcher.*

Left: *The main façade of Colville School.*

Left: *Ladbroke girls in the Fifth and Sixth Form garden of Ladbroke Upper School in St Marks Road. They are: Shirley Hearon, Angela Sheehan, Jennifer Sollis.*

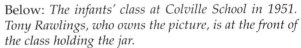

Below: *The infants' class at Colville School in 1951. Tony Rawlings, who owns the picture, is at the front of the class holding the jar.*

LONDON COUNTY COUNCIL

THE COLVILLE J.M. SCHOOL

REPORT FOR YEAR ENDING _July_, 1960.

Name _Maureen Wilkinson_ Number in Class _Year 76_

Class _5_ Position in Class _Year 9_.

SUBJECT		ASSESSMENT	REMARKS
ENGLISH	Oral	good	Maureen's work is good on the whole. Written work needs care
	Written	good	
	Reading	good	
	Compreh.	fair	
ARITHMETIC		good	good class work
HISTORY		good	
GEOGRAPHY		fair	
SCIENCE	Nature	fair	
ART		weak	
WRITING		fair	
HANDWORK	Needlework	Excell.	
OTHER SUBJECTS	P.T.	good.	
	Dancing	good.	

RELIGIOUS KNOWLEDGE............ Attendance _good._
GENERAL REPORT

good on the whole.

Barbara O. Davis Class Master / Class Mistress   _D. Amok_ Head Master / Head Mistress

Above: _Ladbroke School girls on the steps of the dinning-hall. Left to right, standing: Susan Keen, Jean Deveraux, Linda Duddy, Sheila Aylott, Patricia Nurse, Barbara Hunt; middle seated: ?; front seated: Velma John, Pauline Theakston._

Above right: _The dreaded school report in 1960, but for Maureen it was less painful than for me._

Right: _St Stephen's School. Note again the original segregated entrances for girls and boys._

Below: _St Stephen's School, c.1956. Note the white collars. This was a Church of England School with very close links to St Stephen's Church._

Above: Boys from Oxford Gardens School at camp in 1954.

Left: St Stephen's School, Westbourne Park Road.

Below left: Dr Montessori and an unknown child.

Above: Ladbroke School in 1958. The group includes: Margaret Wyse, Valerie Butler, Rosemary Gilfoyle, Miss Hey, Sylvia ?. Note the most fashionable mode of transport in the background – the scooter – just as chic today on the streets of Notting Hill.

toilet block being knocked down, the fabulous Victorian buildings are much the same as they were when I attended. There are still two staircases to the upper floors, one for girls and one for boys, there are signs over the separate gates, again girls and boys and there is still the old laundry block. This was used not only for cleaning any school linen, but in years gone by to teach the female pupils the art of the hand washing of clothes. I'm not sure how the eight or nine year olds of today would react to that kind of lesson. When my sister and I went to Colville the laundry block housed an art class, and is now used as a music suite that is particularly popular with the pupils.

Colville's headmistress in 2006, Mrs Sheila Wiggett.

Having looked around the outside of the school I was taken to the office of the headmistress (Mrs Sheila Wiggett) where I was introduced to two pupils who gave us a tour of the school. Two Year Six pupils escorted Rod Freeman and I around the school, both inside and outside. (Rod Freeman was invaluable during the research of this book. He was my main contact in Notting Hill, and arranged many of my meetings, including this visit to the school. He was the chairman of the PTA, is a familiar face in the area and knows almost everyone with a story to tell. He is also a well-known and successful musician in London.) I left Colville School with a skip in my step and a souvenir – I was given a Colville Primary School mug which will be placed on permanent display in my study.

During 2004 Colville celebrated its 125th anniversary, and to mark the occasion Rod Freeman and the PTA produced a book called *Colville Fusion*. The book contains a mixture of pictures, reminiscences and recipes. The fact that it contains recipes may come as a bit of a surprise, but when you see the book and visit the school you realise the significance. Firstly, to mark the centenary of the school a group of parents, pupils, ex-pupils and staff got together and produced a cookery book – a good idea that would also enhance anything done to mark 125 years. Secondly, the ethnic mix of the school is such that any book containing recipes donated by the children and their parents would be an around-the-world food trip, and indeed it is. There is spicy curry from Bangladesh, pasta from Italy, couscous from Morocco, tadgine from Algeria and, to wash it down, mint tea or Bess Gordon's shave ice cups.

In the years since the centenary the technology for producing the book has changed – whereas the original book would have been painstakingly typed on a typewriter, the 125th-anniversary book was produced on a home PC, something we all take for granted in these days of rapidly improving technology, a technology the young of Colville School take in their stride.

Of course Colville is not the only primary school

in the area, and if you visit Notting Dale, and in particular the Avondale Park area, you will find another school almost made from the same mould. Avondale Park Primary School is also housed in a substantial red-brick Victorian building, and it has all the facilities that are found in modern schools and, like most schools these days, it has its own website.

Then there is Barlby Road and Bevington Road Schools, and Oxford Garden, all of which perform an admirable job of educating the young of the area.

Unfortunately some of the secondary schools of the area disappeared with the slum clearance or re-organisation of schooling in the area. Names such as Portobello School, later to be Isaac Newton and Ladbroke Girls' School, have now gone, but are remembered in the memories and photographs of their former pupils.

A more unusual building which is home to a school is the old Franciscan convent in Portobello Road. It is a fabulous building, hidden behind high walls, designed to maintain a barrier between it and the outside world. This is where the Spanish School is held, which nowadays finds itself in the midst of a large Spanish and Portuguese community. Golborne Road and this end of Portobello Road are home to many Spanish shops and businesses, especially tapas bars and restaurants.

Another educational establishment in the locality is the Montessori School in Kensington Park Road. This is also located in a former religious building – the old synagogue. The Montessori School uses a method of education pioneered by Dr Maria Montessori, which centred on 'supporting and observing the natural development of children'. It is believed to help the pupils in the:

... development of creativity, problem solving, social and time management skills, to contribute to society and the environment and to become fulfilled persons in their particular time and place on earth.

Rod Freeman and pupils in the first-floor hall of Colville School.

Above: Fruit and veg from the road side of the stalls.

Left: Bric-a-brac (or are they antiques?), at Portobello Green. Malcolm Ashman finds something of interest.

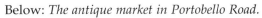

Below: The antique market in Portobello Road.

Chapter 5

The Market Down the Lane

The 'market down the Lane', or as it is better known Portobello Road Market, is a fascinating part of the borough and a place that I personally grew up in. As a child I worked there to earn a little pocket money.

The market itself has been running since the late 1860s, which was a time when many of the buildings on the road where already built or under construction. By the 1890s the market had grown to such an extent that references to the 'obstruction caused by the size of the costermongers' stalls in Portobello Road' was made in the Vestry notes. The market carried on in this way until the 1920s, when discharged soldiers and sailors set up as market traders and they wanted more than just one day a week of trading. Local shopkeepers and the council fought against weekday markets but lacked any power to prevent the traders operating. In 1927 the London County Council (LCC) gave the metropolitan boroughs the power to licence stationary street traders and to make bylaws controlling street trading, but by this time a daily market had become the norm. Licences issued by the council allowed traders to operate between 8am and 8pm, Monday to Friday, and 8am to 9pm on Saturdays, with stalls being restricted to the east side of the lane between Westbourne Grove and Wheatstone Road. In 2006 the market has expanded further, with trading being conducted from the eastern end of Golborne Road, down Portobello Road to Chepstow Villas.

The market was so popular that it became almost a carnival on Saturday evenings. Sir William Bull wrote in 1923:

... the market thronged like a fair from Cornwall Road [now Westbourne Park Road] *to Bolton Road* [now demolished]. *People overflowed from the pavement so that the roadway was quite impassable for horse-traffic... On the east side were costers' barrows, lighted by flaming naphtha lamps and in the side streets were side-shows.*

I don't know what naphtha lamps smell like but I can remember the warm orange glow and smell of hurricane lamps during winter evenings on the market.

The market as we know it in 2006 can be roughly divided into three sections with the top end, Golborne Road and Portobello Road to Portobello Green, being secondhand goods. In the middle section it is fruit and veg, food, etc., and antiques can to be found at the top end, up as far as Chepstow Villas.

During the research for this book it has been my pleasure to meet some real characters. It was a privilege to talk to these people as some of their families have worked the stalls for generations. I am sure that the proud people of the market would not mind me including a few words from the book by Florence Gladstone entitled *Notting Hill in Bygone Days*, which was published in 1924. Writing about the beginning of the 1900s she recorded:

With the advance in years the means of livelihood in Notting Dale have changed. Pig masters and brick makers no longer exist, railway navvies are gone, even hand laundry work has declined in importance, although great steam laundries still employ a small army of women. Cabmen and horse keepers have largely disappeared. The men now chiefly work in factories or as casual labourers in various trades, whilst many manage to earn a livelihood as costermongers, rag and bone men, street hawkers, flower sellers and ice cream men. To this list must be added professional cadgers, thieves, corner men and other professions of a less reputable character.

I hoped things have improved somewhat since those days when Florence Gladstone wrote of the poorer parts of Notting Dale – mainly the Latimer and Norland areas – and to that end I made an effort to catch up with some of the latter-day costermongers. I met up with one ex-stallholder at his home and had a long and very interesting chat about the old days in the market. Albert Peppiat started working in markets when he was ten years old and was a stallholder on the Portobello Road for 40 years. He has worked with fruit and veg and for many of those 40 years bought and sold secondhand goods and antiques. Albert recalled:

Albert Peppiat, October 2005.

Above left: *Portobello Green, sells clothes among many other things. The stallholder looks particularly relaxed and the jacket definitely brings back memories of the swinging '60s.*

Above: *The tented market at Portobello Green.*

Left: *Dunworth Mews, home of the fruit and veg barrows at night.*

Below: *Fruit and veg in Portobello Road. The name on the stall is Cain, an old and well-established family of market traders.*

Portobello Road in the 1950s.

[I remember] *the early Saturday mornings when the stallholders were able to set up their stalls at 4.30am and the buying and selling amongst the stallholders would begin.* [The rules and regulations that are now in place have changed and the traders are not allowed to set up until 5.30am and start trading at 7.30 or 8am.] *In the old days there were the regular stall-holders that would have the same pitch week in week out and the floaters who would be allowed to take the pitches left over. The market inspector would always make sure the regulars were in the same place in the market and would wait near the pitch of a latecomer to make sure he could get in his spot. The system is not as easy now for the 'casuals' – the rules and regulations are such that you need so much documentation and a valid traders' licence that it's impossible to trade on a casual basis.*

One particular type of stallholder was the 'totter', someone like a rag-and-bone man who would go around collecting old and unwanted items from the area through the week and on Saturday would set up a stall and sell the goods. Albert recalled one totter who would:

... drive his horse and cart up the Portobello Road and the horse would know where to stop because he had a regular pitch, his mother Rose would be there waiting with the stall set up and awaiting the stock to arrive.

Prior to the start of the day's trading the stallholders and totters would do a bit of trading amongst themselves and Albert recalls vividly:

One person that seemed to get the pick of the goods was a Mr West – I couldn't understand why at first and got quite upset at the situation. I queried why he was always first to get the pick of the good items – clearly there was a pecking order and Mr West was at the head of the queue. It was a number of years before I reached that level in the hierarchy and before I did Mr West pulled me to one side and said one day you will be in this position – he was right. It is unfortunate that now this sort of respect has gone and these days its just 'first come first served'. There was always certain amount of

loyalty and respect even though earning the money was the reason for being there.

A regular sight in the market were the nuns from the convent who, even though they didn't have a pitch or a stall, would sell goods in the market. The nuns would open the doors of the convent and set up a table just inside. From this vantage point the sisters could do a roaring trade. It must have been an unusual sight to see the sisters competing with the market traders.

Some of the families that have been stallholders for many years are still trading in the market – with names such as Strutton and Worley. Albert recalled that the Worleys had about five stalls on the market. 'The Worleys were on the market for many years and at times probably had at least three generations on stalls.' The Worleys where totters and had horses stabled in the Walmer Road area.

The art of totting is more difficult these days, mainly because there is not the availability of goods and because everyone's an 'expert' when it comes to antiques. You never see the horse and carts around these days. Albert believes that the car-boot fair, along with the high cost of renting a stall, has killed this type of trade. Albert recalls that when he was trading:

... the stall cost around £5 to £6 but this has risen to about £75 and on top of that you have to have insurance etc. It makes it a lot harder to earn enough money to live on from a single day at the market.

In the market there was always a lot of shouting and rivalry for customers and to have a good display, particularly in the fruit and veg market. Albert went on to talk about his time selling more perishable goods:

The fruit and veg side of the market is different because although Saturday was the big day some stalls were on the market through the week. With fruit and veg you had to go to Covent Garden for 4am to buy your stock then bring it back to Portobello Road before start of trading – this meant very early starts. It was very important to get the stalls set out right and we had to polish the brass scales' pan and buff up the apples for display. The boxes of oranges, etc., would be placed just right with some of the fruits wrapped in tissue paper. I do wonder whether it is worth it these days, because with all the traffic it would be impossible to guarantee getting back in time for the start of trading.

With more immigrants in the area the type of fruits and veg on the market became more exotic, and now with people going on long-haul holidays everyone is getting a taste for unusual food, but moreover they want it all year round.

The market traders had language of their own. Everyone knows a bit of cockney rhyming slang but what about 'back slang' or 'A slang'? These are much harder to learn and to listen to when you

Above: *You need a break from a hectic day shopping, even if you are in a pushchair.*

Right: *One man and his dog.*

Cheese and sausages in Portobello Road come with a French accent.

Above: *This CD/DVD stall is located under the A40(M) Westway flyover, nice when it is raining.*

Left: *Dean Wilkinson takes a look at antiques on a stall near Lonsdale Road, March 2006.*

The baguettes must be good if the attention the film crew is giving this stall in Golborne Road is anything to go by. The monolith in the background is Trellick Tower.

A sign of the times. Oysters were a particularly cheap and popular food in the early 1900s.

Hugh Grant's shop from the film Notting Hill *in the antiques section of Portobello Road.*

are unfamiliar with them. Try some back slang and you soon learn that many words do not roll off the tongue when put back to front. Just take 'back' for example – it's not 'kcab', it would be pronounced 'kay cab'. As Albert remembered:

By using our own language we could talk about punters even if they were within earshot, especially the awkward ones. I remember one lady that wanted a pound of apples, trouble was three was just under and four was just over – the old girl wanted the extra weight at the pound price. Thing was she had the wrong attitude and was getting all high and mighty. The problem was solved by cutting one in half – she wasn't well pleased!

Albert blames the local council for the continuing decline in the market:

All the rules and regulations along with them making it impossible to park for both traders and customers is making the market less attractive. Portobello Road market will go the same way as Norland Market – lost for ever along with its characters, character and history.

Albert certainly loved his years as a market trader – he must have done to have lasted as long as he did. He went on to tell me how proud he is to know three or four generations of some market families.

As Albert mentioned Portobello Road was not the only market in the area, and in fact Portobello Road as we know it in 2006 was two distinct markets. Golborne Road was one market and Portobello was another. It was the latter expanding to meet the former, and the addition of the part from Westbourne Grove to Chepstow Villas, that created the market that we now know. The top end of the market which is today's antiques market, has seen the greatest success. It went from being a few stalls and shops in the 1960s to consisting of some 1,500 traders. Many of the shops have been converted into arcades with a myriad of small stalls or kiosks selling all and sundry. Although the shops are open six days a week the market stalls in general are still a Saturday-only phenomenon. The stalls set up early on Saturday morning with trading

starting at about 5.30am, when much of the activity is between dealers from both the UK and overseas. By 8am most of the stalls are set up and general trading gets into full swing. The volume of visitors to the area never seems to be hindered by inclement weather, and indeed the throng and buzz of the tourists and bargain hunters is a year-round happening. In general the antique traders are members of the Portobello Road Antique Dealers Association (PADA), with its members subscribing to a code of practice. The chairman of PADA is Costas Kleanthous who himself runs a shop near Lonsdale Road.

In the Norland area of the borough another market could once also be found. Norland Market was located in Norland Road along with the Sunday 'rag fairs' in Crescent Street and Bangor Street, but these have long-since gone.

Of course not everyone associated with or who visits the markets is a street trader. Jennifer Williams now lives in Wales but in the late 1950s and early '60s she lived just off Talbot Road and went to Colville School. She has some vivid memories of the market:

The market is split into three well-defined areas, the top end is the junk market where just about anything could turn up. I remember my father buying a pair of leather aircraft seats and bringing them home. He put a base on them and we used them as a settee. Then on another occasion he brought home a set of antlers which my mother refused to have in the flat. My father said I should ask the school if they wanted them and they were only too happy to receive them and they were put up in the library. They stayed there ages and in fact were still there when I left to go to Ladbroke. The best time down the Lane was when the mods were about, the unwanted clothes turned out by the old people were at that time sought after by the young people because they had become fashionable again, and they were cheap too. After the mods there were the hippies and again the old stuff on the junk stalls became fashionable, especially the old military uniforms – the long-haired boys would pay good money for an old great coat, unfortunately as soon as the better-off youngsters from Chelsea and South Kensington got into the stuff the prices rocketed – still that's market forces for you.

Chapter 6

Notting Hill Folk;
Up Hill and Down Dale

I really didn't know what to call this chapter and indeed where to put it in the book, but here goes. I use the term 'Notting Hill Folk' to cover both residents of Notting Hill and Notting Dale, but in days gone by the characters of both the area and inhabitants were like chalk and cheese. Over the decades the poorer area (Dale) has seen programmes of slum clearance and social improvement, while the more affluent area (Hill) started to decay and decline in prosperity. At some point both areas became equal, the wealth and social elevation of the area reaching new heights in the 1990s. It is this parity which we see in 2006, with very wealthy and very poor living almost side by side. The large Victorian villas command high prices, as do the smaller mews dwellings or artisan's terrace cottages. As with all properties in the area within any terrace, square or mews, you will find privately-owned, rented, sub-divided and council or housing-association dwellings, which makes it almost impossible to discern any economical divides. This is, it has to be said, good for the harmony of this melting pot we call North Kensington.

Notting Hill folk in my mind are the people who were born and brought up in the area. Very often they are the descendants of the pig farmers, gypsies, totters, artisans and craftsmen that inhabited this part of London from the mid- to late-nineteenth century. They are people who have lived through the bad times of poverty, war and disease. They have enjoyed the community spirit that is found so often in deprived areas; they are very often those people that have found themselves in Notting Hill for the same reason – it was the best they could afford or were offered.

It was, for a long time, a dumping ground for those that no one else wanted or could provide for. Whether they have been in W11 for a number of generations or

are the offspring of migrants, it is their love of Notting Hill that makes these people Notting Hill folk.

When I have approached people to ask them about their lives and living in Notting Hill it is difficult to find a starting point. Tony Rawlings's reply was:

There is so much to tell, what do you want to hear about. I knew of thieves, abortionists, hard-working people, dossers, loose women, stallholders and I even went in to No. 10 Rillington Place a few days after the bodies were removed.

Jennifer Williams (née Sollis) was another – her list of possible subjects read like a who's who of 1950s and '60s London life – 'our landlord was Peter Rachman with his rent collector Michael de Freitas and Christie worked in our local cinema. Tom Jones was our neighbour'. However, the people who are telling these stories were the ordinary people of Notting Hill.

As I have said I have had the pleasure of meeting some fantastic people in conducting my research for this book, but little did I know as I started that I would be turning the tables on a person whose name kept cropping up as someone who could help me. I found his name in books, on websites and even in documentaries on the television. Eddie Adams is probably the foremost authority on Notting Hill and its history. As soon as I met him I was impressed with his warm and friendly manner. He invited me in and immediately took an interest in what I was doing. Eddie must have spoken to hundreds of people over the years, asking questions and documenting their responses, but this time I was there to get his memories. Eddie can take up the story:

I was born in 1936 and lived at 281 Westbourne Park Road from then until 1969 when I moved down to

The fine Victorian dwellings of Lansdowne Crescent.

More fine houses in Lansdowne Road.

Above left: *Westbourne Park Road. These houses are at the eastern end of the road.*

Above: *Former totters' houses in St Lukes Mews.*

Left: *Kensington Park Road. The shop on the right-hand corner was, for a number of years, Barnetts toy shop.*

A community gets together in Walner Road to celebrate the coronation of Queen Elizabeth in 1952.

(PICTURE COURTESY OF EDDIE ADAMS)

Cornwall Crescent, which is the continuation of Westbourne Park Road but on the other side of Ladbroke Grove. After that we, my wife and I, moved up to W10.

I have some vivid memories of the war years, not least of all the time we had to stay with friends because a doodlebug [German V1 flying bomb] dropped just up the road where Clydesdale House is now located. It was 1944, we were all indoors when the bomb landed between Powis Gardens and Clydesdale Road. It was incredible – all our doors and windows were blown in, there was glass and wood everywhere. It was surprising none of the ceilings came down, but we did have a job finding the cat and dog – they were OK, we found the cat and her kittens covered in glass on one of the armchairs with no injuries whatsoever. The damage to the property meant that my family and the other residents of the house had to find a bed else where for a few days. Mind you we were the lucky ones – 21 other residents were killed. We stayed in Elgin Crescent with friends. We quite enjoyed it, it was really quite exciting for us as kids. I remember walking along Portobello Road and seeing all the stock from the shops on the road because the bombs had blown it all out of the broken windows. My father told us not to touch anything because of the looting laws that were enforced. I can remember the entire family in the tobacconist's shop being killed by the bombing. Scotchbrook was their name. I have to say that because of the rationing the kids would always be looking around for sweets and stuff we could liberate, but we had to be careful.

[Eddie went on to tell me that he was evacuated twice during the war]... the first time I was sent down to Roadwater in Somerset which I enjoyed but came back to London for a while before being sent to Lancashire later on during the war.

My father worked on aircraft production in Swindon – he was an electrician and had been sent to Swindon under wartime direction of labour. My mother was ill so being evacuated was the only option we had. When I came back to London I lived with my aunt, but unfortunately my mother died in 1941. My aunt lived in Winterbourne Buildings in Notting Dale where I stayed for a while, then spent time at home when my father came back to London because of the family situation.

I can also remember another lady that lived upstairs, Mrs James, going to the mobile first-aid station after an air raid. She only had dust in her eyes but while she was waiting the adjacent bomb-damaged building collapsed on to the first-aid station – which was ironic – but she was unhurt thankfully.

Eddie also went to Colville School. He started at the age of six or seven during the war.

I was happy to get involved with the 125th anniversary celebrations for the school in 2004 and am proud that the school is still going strong, unlike many of the other early School Board schools in the area. I wrote about my years at Colville and reminisced about playing on the

bomb site opposite. It's where the flats are now. The teachers would tell us how dangerous it was but we were young and kids will be kids. On another occasion I was going to a school party, I took half a crown (12½ pence) from home and bought a paper admiral's hat from Barnetts. I really thought I was the cat's whiskers but I paid for it when I got home I can tell you.

I can remember Guy Fawkes night, especially in Basin Street – all the locals would collect old wood and stuff and build a huge bonfire in the road. It was quite a sight. Everyone brought fireworks to let off but eventually the fire brigade would come to put it out, not till late though. The following day the council would clear up the debris and usually had to arrange for the road to be resurfaced because of the heat.

Tony Rawlings lives at Truro, Cornwall now but he is a North Kensington man through and through, as indeed was his father before. In fact they are from Notting Dale and Tony is a veritable mine of information and stories about the area. I made contact with Tony through the website 'Friends Reunited', mainly because of a photo he had posted on the Colville School section. Tony continues with his story:

I was born in 1947 at 192 Kensington Park Road the second of three children. The flat was just two rooms on the top floor with no kitchen, no electricity or bathroom. There was only one toilet and that was under the stairs two floors down. On the ground floor was a grocer's shop. However, my parents and the doctors didn't think I was going to see the house because I was very ill at birth – so ill that I was put on what they called open orders, no one thought I would make it. My parents decided that I should be baptised straight away just in case, so my baptism certificate reads that I was baptised at St Charles Hospital, as most places in them days St Charles had a nickname – to the locals it was known as the 'death house'. I guess I was lucky I had a fantastic doctor, Dr Hennigan he was called. Even after I went home he carried on looking after me. Trouble was my parents had to pay half a crown per visit – sometimes Dr Hennigan didn't take the money – he knew how poor the family was. Because of my ill health I had to be

Melvin Wilkinson and Jackie Rawlings search for old pictures in 2005.

Tony Rawlings being held by his parents at the Blenheim Pub in 1950.

Arthur Harwood, Tony Rawlings, David Harwood and Tony's sister Jessica outside 192 Kensington Park Road in 1956.

weighed every day but we didn't have any scales so my Dad bought a set down the lane [Portobello Market] from a secondhand stall. They were like the ones you weigh out fruit and veg in, I know because I remember them still in the cupboard when I was about ten. The second of the Rawlings family to be born at 192 Kensington Park Road was my sister Jessica. Unlike me she was born healthy which meant that all five of us lived in two rooms, but we managed OK. Oh, I forgot to say my brother Dennis was born in Acklam Road. I think it was the norm in those days to be born at home.

As I grew up there was a group of us kids that always went around together. I can remember the others now. There was Arthur and David Harwood, Malcolm Morrison (his Dad owned the pet shop in Blenheim Crescent and he was the first person I knew with a television), then there was Colin Hinton. I haven't seen any of them apart from Malcolm since I left 192 in 1958.

We were tearaways I suppose but, I was thinking back, even though we were poor we had standards. I mean we lived over Doris Sanderson's grocers shop. In the communal hallway she would stack stock but no one stole any, even if we were desperate my parents would always ask Doris for goods on tick [credit].

Tony has already been researching his family history and has traced his family tree back to the mid-1800s, and in researching has turned up some interesting details, the highlights of which Tony told me:

I have researched my family tree back to 1837 so far which equates to about six generations. From the addresses alone I can tell my ancestors were from the poorer members of the community, so I'll start with my great-great-grandfather Thomas Rawlings, who was born in 1836. He lived at 371 Portobello Road when he married for the second time after being widowed. Thomas and his new wife Jane (Dumont) had a son Thomas (junr) who, when he married Ester (May) in

1893 was living at No. 4 Threshers Cottages. They also had a son Harry (b.1900) who was born at No. 17 Tobin Street, which really was in the heart of Notting Dale – at the time the very poorest part of the area, so poor that the road had its own soup kitchen. Harry's father Thomas died of TB which meant that his wife and five children were left in poverty. Harry and his brother William were sent to a home for the Poor Law boys in Hayes, Middlesex. William hated the home so lied about his age and signed up for the army. William, or Bill as he was known, joined the Seaforth Highlanders and was killed on active service in Iraq during the First World War.

My father George Rawlings was born in 1921 in a tenement block in Talbot Grove, still even at that time a particularly run-down area. He married my mother Barbara and in turn they had three children – my elder brother Dennis who was born in Acklam Road myself and my younger sister Jessica, both of who were born in 192 Kensington Park Road. To bring the story up to date I have one son Tom who at the time of writing is 21. That's not the entire family mind, there were other branches of the family via marriage. My favourite was my Uncle Jeffery 'Buffy' Blakelock – Buffy was a nickname which came about because of his weight at birth. Buffy weighed 13 pounds 10 ounces when born and when his father Bert was chatting to local boxer Alf Mancini he told him of his son's weight – Alf replied with some expletives 'that aint a baby that's a buffalo', and the name stuck. My maternal great-grandfather was a well-known swordsmith who worked for Wilkinson Sword. His name was Tom Beasley, and for years he lived in West London, having moved down from Birmingham. I'm proud to say he featured on a cigarette card issued by Churchmans.

Another thing that particularly sticks in my mind is the holidays we had in the old days. They weren't like the holidays you have today – we used to go hop picking in Kent. We had a fantastic time; we spent the days picking hops into hessian bags, for which we got paid one shilling

Above: *An early cigarette card featuring Tony Rawlings's ancestor, Thomas Beasley.*

Right: *A young Jessica Rawlings on a hop-picking holiday in 1955.*

Above: *Members of the Rawlings family outside the huts on the hop farm in Kent.*

Left: *Tony Rawlings outside 192 Kensington Park Road in 2005.*

a bushel. The evenings were spent entertaining ourselves, playing games and having a singsong in the huts – they certainly were good times. I remember a couple of days before coming home we went scrumping in the farmer's orchard. We had to be careful to keep the apples out of sight when we went home on the lorry though.

When I was ten I got a job down the Lane [Portobello Road] working on a stall. Ted Waitlin owned the stall, he was a nice bloke. I worked on a Saturday collecting stock from the lock up, clearing up at the close of business and helping to pull the stall back to the lock up. I remember people picking up the specky fruit and veg that was discarded in the gutter. There was [sic] also a few old soldiers still about at the time, they usually had a disability like an arm or a leg missing so they would sell boxes of matches from a tray around their necks. There was [sic] still a lot of poor people about even then.

All in all I enjoyed my life and the freedoms we had as children, working down the Lane, playing on the bomb sites and getting around parts of the area or even going as far as Hampstead Heath, Kensington Gardens or the museums in Kensington. We all survived and grew up OK.

From all that Tony has relayed to me for this portion of the book one thing that has come across is that whatever the conditions of the accommodation, however hard up the people and however difficult it was for them to lead a reasonable life, there was still a pride inside. We all, as Notting Hill folk, enjoyed ourselves and were grateful for whatever we had. Tony is proud of his upbringing at 192 Kensington Park Road, and quite rightly too, but I wonder what he would have said back then if he had been told that Doris Sanderson's grocers shop would, some 50 years on, be a wine bar that would feature so prominently in a blockbuster film – *Bridget Jones' Diary*. The images of then and now are poles apart.

Talking to Tony has made me think back to my early years and especially to the holidays we would go on. I think we were fairly lucky compared to many, and unlike Tony and his family we didn't have

to work through the days on hop farms. It wasn't foreign holidays either. My family and sometimes my grandfather would go to Clacton or the Isle of Sheppey where we would hire a chalet for a week. The chalets were small, usually just two rooms and no bath or shower – those facilities were in a communal block elsewhere on the site, but we enjoyed it. Even getting there was an adventure. We went by coach from Victoria and the coach company was called 'Grey Green Coaches'. It was always a rush to get the back seats.

The other thing that comes across from my research is the respect and love people had for their family. This is something that was always seen at Christmas and other occasions. Family gatherings in Notting Hill were special occasions when all branches and parts of the extended family would be represented, and of course the spirits would usually be raised with copious quantities of alcohol and homemade food. Parties or gatherings at private addresses would usually go on until the early hours.

Maureen Marshall remembers the Household Cavalry passing under her bedroom window early on Sunday mornings:

Sunday mornings were always lie-in mornings but on some of those Sundays there would be the sound of hooves on the tarmac of Westbourne Park Road. For someone that would only see horses in the flesh on very rare occasions it was a sound that would wake me and draw me to the windows no matter how early or how cold it was. We didn't have double glazing in those days so in the winter I would have to scrape the ice off of the inside of the glass, but through the glass I would get a fabulous view of the troopers and their mounts heading for Wormwood Scrubs for some practice or exercise. On some days they would be in full dress uniform and even have their cannons and limbers – it was a fabulous sight.

On other occasions I can remember seeing paratroops also practising on Wormwood Scrubs, not just one or two but hundreds and with our flat roof we could see the

Maureen and Melvin Wilkinson on holiday in Clacton with their parents Kathleen and Alfred, and grandfather Harry Harris, c.1960.

Christopher Russell, Susan Parry and other pupils from Colville Junior Mixed School at the school camp in 1962.

Above: *All aboard! The Notting Barn Tavern annual outing in the 1920s, outside Hooper and Hawkins, Silchester Road.*
(PICTURE COURTESY OF EDDIE ADAMS)

Right: *Georgina, Charles and Rosina Sayle outside No. 42 St Lawrence Terrace in 1946.*

Below right: *The junction of Golborne Road and Bevington Road. Note the underground public conveniences on the island in the middle of the road.*

Below: *The wedding of Johnny Brazier and Nellie Chamberlain in 1946. The picture was taken in the square of Princess Alice House, W10.*

planes dropping the soldiers and even the old barrage balloons they used sometimes. It was very interesting to watch.

Unfortunately Notting Hill is an area that people come into, stay a while and then move on again, and even many of the old-established families with roots going back 100 years or more in the area have finally moved on. Many of those families were the ordinary and poor families that would have occupied the slum areas of the district, their migration often being brought about by the slum clearance of the 1960s and the construction of the Westway and consequential loss of working-class housing. One such person is John Kinman who now lives in Eastcote, Middlesex:

I lived in Acklam Road which of course was swept away with the construction of the Westway. It was a very poor area and the housing was very shabby, but I still look back with a great deal of fondness. There was always a sense of community, neighbours would always help each other out. It was quite a wrench when we moved even though I was quite young at the time.

I still go back to the area on a regular basis and even popped into my old school last time I was there. I went to Bevington Road School which is just off Golborne Road and have fond memories of my time there. When I went back I don't think I was ready for how I felt. I got quite emotional, I think it is because between the ages of five or six and 11 years you are particularly impressionable.

Anyway I hadn't been invited in so I just took a quick look around and then left, but the funny thing was when I left I looked around and all the old feelings and memories came flooding back. Just across the road from the school was a rag-and-bone shop and as kids we would collect all the old clothes and stuff and bag it up to sell to the rag man. We would load it up on an old pram or pushchair and go off to the rag man to sell it. He had a set of old balance scales which he weighed the rags on and then paid you by the weight. It was something that all the kids of the area did but I suspect

that, like me, the other kids didn't have a clue how much per pound he paid – trouble was he could move the counter balance weights back and forth so fast you couldn't keep up with him. We only got a few coppers but we thought we were well off for a while. The other thing I remember is the public conveniences at the junction of Bevington Road and Golborne Road. They were underground and were fully tiled with polished copper pipes. They are still there but I don't think they are open now. On Golborne Road there was a Post Office and further up towards the railway bridge Harpers the toy shop, then there was the pie and mash shop and Holmes the bakers.

As kids we spent loads of time in the pie and mash shop, it was cheap and even at only seven or eight our parents would send us off to get our dinner in there. Holmes the bakers made their own bread on the premises so you could get warm bread in the morning – that smell of fresh bread was out of this world and there is nothing like warm crusty bread.

In 1958 there was a murder outside the Earl of Warwick which is on the corner of Southam Street and Golborne Road. It is particularly memorable because it shook the whole community, both black and white. The victim was a black man called Kelso Cochram. He was killed by a group of white males who were never caught – I think that after the riots this was an incident that no one wanted. It was a wake-up call for both black and white communities.

I remember several films that were shot in the area. There was The Blue Lamp *which was filmed in Ladbroke Grove over the old iron bridge, then they filmed in Bramley Road. It was always interesting to see places you know on the big screen.*

John is clearly proud of his roots and, like myself, still thinks of Notting Hill as his home, even though he has been away longer than he actually lived there – 'it's where the heart is' he added, 'I was christened in All Saints Church and still have the certificate to prove it, so I think that really makes me one of the Notting Hill folk.'

Tony Allen, local comedian, speaker and anarchist.

John Kinman, November 2005.

Eddie Adams, local historian and archivist.

The cast of the Bevington Road School nativity play in the 1950s. John Kinman is in the back row, seventh from the left.

Chapter 7

Londoners – From the World Over

The mix of races, creeds, nationalities and lifestyles in the Notting Hill area is not a new phenomenon. Almost from its earliest days, the ethnic mix has made the area colourful, exciting, energetic and at times downright dangerous.

So who were and are the people of Notting Hill? We can go as far back as the Romans in about AD100 when two important roads passed through or very close to Notting Hill. The roads were Watling Street, heading north from London, and the Great West Road, heading out towards Wales in the west. The importance of the roads can be measured by the fact that our modern road systems follow these great military arteries of some 1,900 years ago. Watling Street is overlaid by Edgware Road and the Great West Road by parts of Oxford Street and Bayswater Road. Even though the Romans would have been familiar with Notting Hill it seems that they merely passed through it, or close by. This is demonstrated by the fact that no Roman artefacts have been found within the borough, with the exception of what was believed to be a stone sarcophagus, which was found in the mid-1800s while foundations were being built for No. 1 Ladbroke Square. Although Londinium became important in the Roman empire, the people were not sure if the rough residents of London were native or barbarians that had found their way to this settlement over hundreds of years. What is certain is that the Romans would not be the last migrants to visit this part of England.

It was in about AD700, some 450 years after the Roman departure, that the Saxons made their presence felt in the dale and hills, with London being considered the capital of the East Saxon Kingdom of what is now known as Essex. Indeed the very names Notting Hill and Kensington are believed to originate from the Saxon period, although notable historians and scholars do not always agree on the exact origin. I think it important that conflicting theories be documented and the reader left to decide which fits the bill best, or has a more romantic tone. It is said that the earliest form of Kensington was derived from Saxon immigrants known as 'the Sons of Cynesige'. These settlers built their 'tun' or village on the raised lands above the marshlands along the Thames. So it was that the name Chenesitun was born. Notting Hill was similarly derived from the settlers called the Cnottingas, or 'sons of Cnotta'. However, there is another theory that it is derived from the followers of King Knut (albeit that King Knut was a Dane), or even from the nut bushes that grew on the slopes of the hill.

Further more it was even suggested that the name is a corruption of 'Nothing Ill'. The closest version to the present name appeared in 1361 when Knottynghull was recorded on the patent roll for that year.

As we have noted people came and went – Romans, Saxons, Vikings and so on – but it was not until the mid-1800s that migrants arrived who would make a solid and tangible lasting impression on Notting Hill that is present there in 2006. They arrived from Ireland as 'navvies' to build the railways that would cut across the area. The West London Railway, the Hammersmith and City and of course the Great Western Railway brought armies of Irish workers into the area. The migrant workers settled in the few streets that existed in the Latymer Junction area of the Piggeries part of Notting Dale.

Many of the Irish stayed once the railway was complete and settled in the poor areas. The workers were followed to Notting Hill by other family members who felt compelled to try their luck in Notting Hill. The Irish were joined on a seasonal basis to start with by the Romany gypsies who would set up their caravan villages or 'gypseries' on the then open spaces of Notting Dale. They came in late spring for the fairs, circuses and carnivals that provided an income for a few months. So many came that the gypseries were the biggest in London and, even as the years went on and many took to living in houses, the caravans remained. The presence of some caravans was recorded as late as 1881. Life in the Potteries and Piggeries was hard and the inhabitants found many different ways of making money – a few of which were legal and a lot of which were not.

Colville Mews.

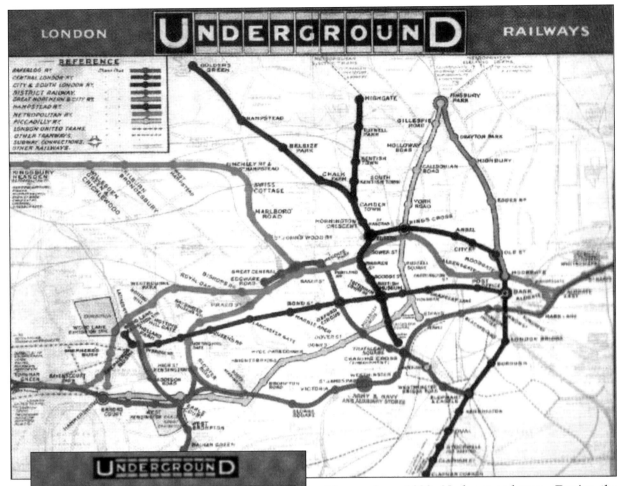

Above: *A pre-1930s Underground map. During the 1930s Henry Beck designed the 'electrical wiring diagram' inspired map that is used to this day.*

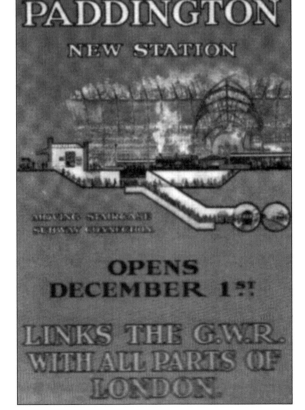

Left: *The opening of Paddington Bakerloo Line Station in 1913. It was the one of the first stations designed with moving staircases.*

Opposite: *A railway map of 1899. Note that Ladbroke Grove Station was then called Notting Hill and Ladbrook Road.*

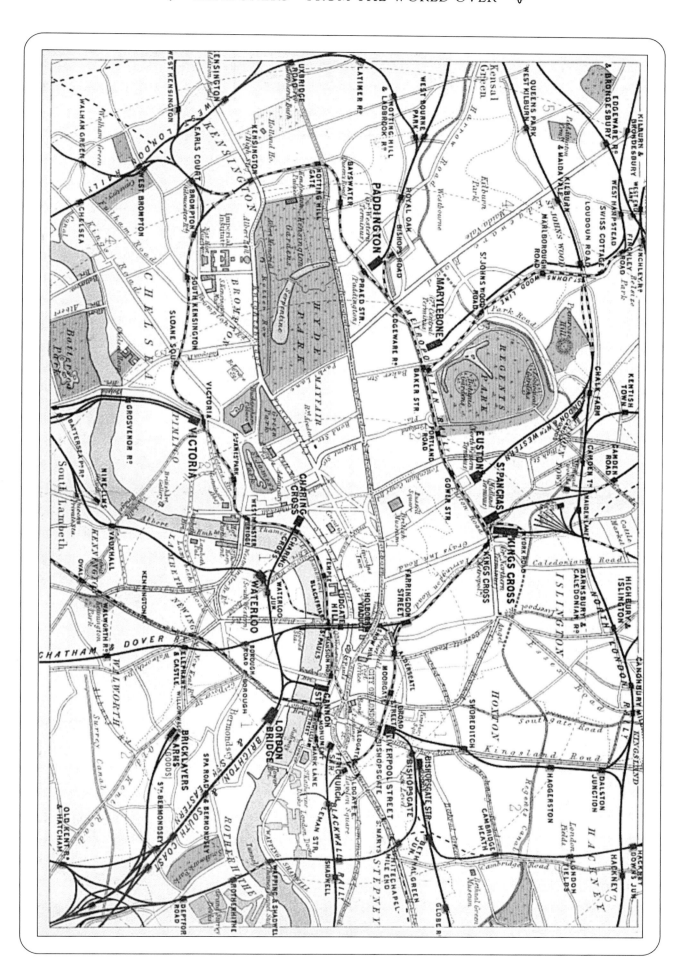

Above: *The entrance to St Lukes Mews.*

Left: *Colville Mews, the site of one of the 'ragged schools' in the area. Many of the ragged-school pupils later went to Buckingham Terrace School.*

Left: *St Columbs in Lancaster Road is used as the Serbian Orthodox Church in 2006.*

Below: *Powis Square in 2005.*

One of the legal ways was working as totters and street traders – the gypsies took to this and the sight of totters' carts drawn by horses was something that survived until very recently, and indeed in some parts totters' horses can still be seen in 2006. The growth in this type of business is reflected in the mews buildings of the area. They typically had living accommodation over a stable or 'lock up' where the horses, cart or stall would be housed. Most of the mews properties have now been converted into luxury accommodation for the well off in the area with the stables now concealing expensive mega horsepower cars instead of an old nag or two.

With the Irish and gypsies now settled as locals, and street markets common, the different tongues that could be heard by the late 1800s and early 1900s was staggering – there were Spanish, eastern Europeans from countries such as Poland, Russia and Hungary, Asians from India, and South Americans. There were Jews, Christians, Muslims and Hindus. Notting Hill was becoming a melting pot, a trait that remains to this day.

The Jewish community in the borough tended to live around the St Lukes Road and Kensington Park Road areas – they brought with them their shops and trades which flourished in and around All Saints Road. The synagogue was in Kensington Park Road and occupied what is now the Montessori School.

In the 1870s, a time when the roads around Notting Hill were still developing – especially the trading centre of Portobello Road – Messrs Walter, Wren and Gurney operated a teaching establishment (later known as the Wren College) in Powis Square. The college prepared young men for higher examinations, mainly for the Indian Civil Service. Because of the volume of students requiring accommodation many of the large houses in the square where turned in to boarding-houses. It was this that led to the small area being nicknamed 'Little India'.

In the Golborne Road area there are large numbers of Spanish people, and indeed the Spanish School which is located in Portobello Road. This is a little ironic really, considering that the road is named after the battle of Puerto Bello of 1739 – the British Navy, and indeed the English people, considered the Spanish their greatest adversaries at the time. The Spanish and Portuguese are now particularly well established and have a thriving community, which became firmly established by refugees fleeing the Spanish Civil War in the 1930s.

In addition to the many Spanish families, most people will probably be unaware that there are also a number of Moroccans living here. The Moroccan community of North Kensington is in fact the largest in England.

The next big influx of immigrants was in the mid-1950s and it is ironic that they too, like the Irish, were invited to these shores in an effort to bolster the workforces. In this case it was as an instant workforce for the railways and buses – they were and are the Afro-Caribbean people that have now made England and Notting Hill their home. They came from Jamaica, Trinidad and all over the West Indies to work on the buses, underground, railways and in hospitals, and they became an invaluable part of the community bringing the laughter, sunshine and song of the Caribbean to a dull and dismal part of London. But life was never easy for our new neighbours. The story of these immigrants is told within other chapters of this book, an indication of how important they were, and are, to the life and livelihood of the borough.

It is not only large volumes of any one nationality that have settled in what is now London W11, but also individuals from many parts of the world, and indeed from other parts of the United Kingdom, that have integrated into this most cosmopolitan of neighbourhoods. People have moved to Notting Hill to start and run businesses, to marry, have families and just to be in an exciting, interesting and vibrant part of London. I have spoken to a number of these people and asked them why they came to Notting Hill, and what attracted them to this part of the United Kingdom. One of these people is Ninon Asuni, who I met at her shop in All Saints Road. Ninon came to England from her native Nigeria in the early part of the 1970s, but it wasn't until 1978 that she finally ended up in Notting Hill:

I had friends in the area and liked its atmosphere. I was fortunate to be offered accommodation so it all seemed to fall into place. I run the bicycle shop which keeps me busy – its a business that I have built up to what it is today.

Ninon lives in a basement in a road off of All Saints Road. The basement flats like Ninon's are quintessentially London and to me very Notting Hill – as a child a number of my friends lived in similar accommodation in similar roads. I asked Ninon how the area has changed and what she loves about it:

When I first came to North Kensington this area was run down, many of the shops were unused and the ones

Ninon Asuni outside her bicycle shop in All Saints Road.

that were used were untidy. Many of the windows had corrugated iron over them, it really looked awful. When I first rented my shop the landlords charged a very low rent because nobody wanted it. I was surprised also to see the houses in the state they were – when you walk down the roads now they are all painted up to look nice but in those days the render was falling off, any painted facades were peeling as if they hadn't been repainted in decades. The housing was mainly privately rented and I guess maintenance was low on the list of priorities for the landlords. As I said nobody owned their homes and privately rented accommodation was poor at best, council accommodation was in short supply so something had to be done. Local pressure groups and activists pressured the authorities to do something about the situation. During this period a number of housing associations were set up and they are now major supplier of accommodation in the area. Their influence can be seen and felt, not only in the greater and better choice of living accommodation, but also in the industrial and retail section where again they have obtained and renovated a number properties. The fact that the shops are being used and are tidy means that the area seems prosperous and vibrant.

Over the years we have seen a number of different nationalities come to the area, of course there are the obvious ones like the West Indians, African and Irish communities but there are also strong Spanish, Moroccan, Polish and now Serbian and Croatian communities – they have all brought something to our part of London. There was a time when some of the young members of the community started getting out of hand and this culminated in the trouble at the carnival a few years ago. I think some good came out of that trouble, it seemed to galvanise the communities and the authorities into action and we addressed the problems. I think it brought our community closer together. However, it was frightening at the time, especially living in a basement. When the riots were in full swing I took refuge in an upper-floor flat in the house – I was afraid that things would be thrown through the windows. Riots definitely look worse when you are looking up at them from a basement!

Although I wasn't here when the Westway extension was pushed through I can see that it has cut the area in half. There are a number of barriers in the locality – the canal and Hammersmith and City line – but the Westway is a real division. It's a high brick wall and you can see and feel the differences that have grown up between the communities on either side. Something that is changing locally is the fact that many houses are now in private ownership again, not for renting but as family homes. I guess the latest influx (over the last ten years or so) of new residents are the 'yuppies' that aspire to live in Kensington. This has pushed the house prices through the roof with terraced properties changing hands for £1 to £1.5 million. I have also felt lately that some of the warmth and sense of community has gone – don't get me wrong, that doesn't mean I love the area any less.

You only have to wander around the area to see the characters that seem to propagate around and about. I am sure that Bess Gordon won't mind me calling her a character because, quite simply, she is. She is a jewel in the area, but who is Bess Gordon? Bess can be found every day outside All Saints Church selling 'shave ice' from her makeshift stall, but I must not minimise what and who Bess is. When I met her she was doing a roaring trade with children and adults alike waiting to buy the cold refreshments. With the customers still coming to buy, Bess handed over the business to her daughter so that we could have a chat:

I came to England in 1957 and have lived in Notting Hill all those years. They were hard times, housing was poor and racism was very much in evidence. By 1958 we saw the race riots in Notting Hill, they certainly weren't pleasant times. In 1966 I started working at Colville School as lunch/classroom supervisor. I can remember in those days the small children in the nursery would have a sleep after dinner. They had small cots that we set out and they would nap for about an hour. I would also talk in morning assembly and would tell the children about my dreams and about when I was a child in Jamaica. I carried on at Colville until 1995 and have seen many children come and go including my own children and grandchildren. It makes me think sometimes, I'm not only a grandmother I'm now a great-grandmother.

I have been selling shave ice outside All Saints church since 1972. I meet all kinds of people out here, old, young, black, white – the spectrum of Notting Hill residents, and in the main they are all so very friendly and polite.

I love Carnival, I have met some lovely people during the bank holiday weekends over the years. It's incredible [that] even with the million or so people that come to Notting Hill for Carnival the same ones come back year after year and say hello as they pass my house. I often get asked by revellers if they can use our toilet or just rest by our front door and they always remember us when they pass by in later years. We have also had some bad times, like when we had riots at Carnival in the 1970s; what came out of it was good though. The organisers do

Bess Gordon adds some flavour to the icy refreshment.

Bess Gordon's shave ice stall outside All Saints Church, ably managed by her daughter.

a fantastic job and the police are now much more sympathetic to the Caribbean culture. It all adds up to a fantastic weekend for all that enjoy Carnival.

Bess is definitely a part of Notting Hill and we must thank Jamaica for her humour, caring nature and talent for imparting the Caribbean sunshine into everyone that meets her. Oh, and if you are wondering, shave ice is like slush puppies but Bess simply has a large block of ice on her barrow which she shaves off manually with a metal scraper and then adds whatever flavour you want.

One person who has been a great help in my research turned out to be another Londoner from elsewhere. Rod Freeman is from the north-east of England, or is a Geordie, as we would affectionately call him. Rod spoke of how he came to be in Notting Hill:

I landed in Notting Hill purely by chance really – following a spell farming in Spain I came back to England and stayed with friends in Plaistow in the east end of London, but really needed to find somewhere of my own. It was about February 1976, I was wandering around the area and just on the off chance asked a chap that was building a wall if he knew of any rooms to rent. He looked me up and down and sent me off to Leamington Road Villas to a guy called Charles Parker who was an opera singer that rented a few rooms out, mainly to musicians like myself. I later found out that the bricklayer was a Polish guy called Joe and I am pleased to say that he is still in the area.

At that time there were a lot of run-down houses in the area and an amazing amount of squatting. I got heavily involved in the setting up of a housing co-operative. Revd Bruce Kenrick, who was an amazing chap, was involved in starting Notting Hill Housing Trust (NHHT) in the '60s and eventually managed to get money from the Housing Corporation to help with renovating properties in the area. W11 Housing Co-operative was formed in 1978 and under a management agreement with NHHT we collected our own rents and were responsible for the external maintenance programme.

I wasn't actually a complete stranger to London or indeed Notting Hill when I came to live here because I

Rod Freeman enjoys a cup of tea in a market-traders' café in Portobello Road.

had been to Portobello Road back in 1959 with my grandmother – she had relations living in Camberwell. We didn't have street markets in the north-east so it was a new experience and an adventure. I remember looking up the roads that run off of Portobello Road – in fact it was probably Lancaster Road that I looked at – and saw shabby and run-down houses. I couldn't believe the appalling state of the properties. Some had boarded-up windows and looked almost derelict, the paint was peeling and the woodwork rotten but people were living in them. I would never have dreamed that later in my life I would be living in this part of London. The housing association and Co-op certainly improved the accommodation situation, mainly because the housing legislation of the day didn't help certain groups of people like singles and students for example, myself included. These groups also tended to be or include musicians, artists and actors, people that didn't have a regular wage, but the Co-op could help them with accommodation.

[Managing in the early days as a musician living in London] was quite simple really – I discovered Portobello Road! First of all I managed to buy all I needed down the market for very little money, I got furniture and nick-nacks, everything to make a flat comfortable. Later on I was offered a stall and would go around during the week looking for stuff to sell on a Saturday. I would ride my bicycle out as far as bits of Middlesex like Twickenham going to jumble sales, mainly looking for 1950s stuff which the yuppies that frequented the market found desirable. I have even been known to ride back with furniture balanced on my bike down the A316 from Chiswick and back home. I did that for some 12 years and really enjoyed it. I met some fantastic people from all over the world.

Of course being a musician I also earned a few bob by playing in the pubs and clubs in the area. I must have played in every licensed bar in the area by now. The area has always been very musical you can find any genre from folk to jazz, reggae and blues – just about everything.

Rod Freeman (guitar) entertains in the Duke of Cornwall on Ledbury Road in 1990.

I remember the free school that was held in the hut in Powis Square. The locals were always suspicious but the main thing was the kids that got help from it, kids that had dropped out for one reason or another and couldn't get educated anywhere else.

So there you have it. I have lived in Notting Hill since 1976 and have really become part of the community, mainly because I have stayed in and around the same roads. I got married in 1990 and have two kids so the only real move was some 100 yards to a larger flat. My children went to Colville School and that led to me being the chair of the PTA which was good. I met lots of people including Eddie Adams who helped me with the 125th anniversary book. We ran summer fairs and the like, which also says a lot about the community spirit because we always got fantastic support from community leaders and local residents for anything we did. The other thing is that the school has tended to be a central contact point for many of the new immigrants that come to the area. Over the time that I have been involved with the PTA it has been [people from] Kosovo and Croatia that have come here with their children and we all helped them in whatever way we could. But that has been the same with all the different ethnic groups – the community opens up and accepts them.

There isn't really a downside [to living in the area] now. There was in the 1980s when the drug gangs seemed to run All Saints Road, but again the community got together and did something about it. The police at that time were very heavy-handed, which wasn't the right approach, so in the end local community leaders and prominent figures got together with the police to get the problem sorted out, and I think that by and large it has been a success.

I love West 11 – it kind of creeps up on you and the next thing you know you're a local.

It's not every day you meet someone that has been described thus: 'He is a brilliant stand-up comedian

A poster advertising just one of the many shows that have included the talent of Tony Allen.

and seminal figure in the history of British comedy.' The bravery and inventiveness of his work has led comedians to describe him as 'the Master', while *The Independent* newspaper called him 'a sell-out alternative who has not sold out.' The man is Tony Allen, a particularly laid back and well-known member of the Notting Hill community.

The first thing Tony did was to try to help with suggestions of people I should talk to in my quest for the real people of Notting Hill. The suggestions came thick and fast and, in between the names of journalists, radio broadcasters and local characters, his dexterity on the computer was displayed as he surfed the web for the contact details of anyone that could help to fill the chapters of this book with anecdotes and stories. It has to be said that he wasn't trying to discharge any obligation he may have felt he had, but his real effort to help and be part of a project related to the community he undoubtedly loves and is part of.

Tony was born in Hayes, Middlesex, with his father originally coming from Shepherd's Bush. He was based in a squat in the Harrow Road area for a while before migrating southwards into North Kensington. He has been an anarchist for a number of years and is billed as a mixed-ability shaman. He has spent many a Sunday at speakers' corner and even managed to get an Arts Council grant during the 'Year of the Artist' to be an 'advocate heckler at

Maureen Wilkinson and Susan Parry stand across the road from the Apollo pub, All Saints and Lancaster Roads, in the early 1960s.

All Saints Road from Cornwall Terrace (later Westbourne Park Road) in the early 1900s.

Speakers' Corner'. I have to confess that I was a little sceptical about this when I read it in his book, *A Summer in the Park,* so I did what any good investigator would do – I asked him, 'Oh yes it's true, all of it, every word' was his response.

Tony went on to relate a tale that sums up himself and the feelings in the community at a difficult and worrying time:

I think I had been playing at a local pub or somewhere and was on my way home with a colleague, Danny. We rode our bikes up Tavistock Road and turned right into All Saints Road, at the time a notorious drug-dealing road with drug busts a regular occurrence. Well, a drug bust is exactly what was going down on the junction with Lancaster Road. A panda car was placed to create a road block and a number of police officers were trying their hardest to contain the somewhat anxious crowd that was gathering. The crowd was watching the police carry out the business of searching three black youths who had been made to 'assume the position' against the tiled walls of the then boarded up Apollo pub. The crowd was in a state of agitation with antagonism and comments flying, until Danny and I ride into the middle of the junction playing kazoos and singing the middle eight of 'Somewhere Over the Rainbow', with simulated police sirens and 'someday I'll wish upon a star and wake up where the clouds are far behind me blah blah blah' being sung out at the top of our voices. It was at this point we both leapt off our bikes and joined the line of suspects – we then in turn 'assumed the position' and took it in turns to frisk each other whilst maintaining the most suitable sound effect for the situation in hand, then with outstanding timing and pockets still inside out we mounted our bikes and sped the 20 or so yards to my flat. There was a dumbfounded silence that spoke volumes and then applause, followed by general laughter from the crowd. The police seemed to have a sense of

disbelief that this could be happening, could happen and indeed had happened.

Although we hadn't set out to achieve it many of my neighbours thanked me later, apparently for making a statement on behalf of the local community both against the drug gangs and the police snatch squads. There was something else that happened that day – I felt connected to the ancient art of foolery, and that really felt good.

Jennifer Williams (née Sollis) has particularly fond memories of Notting Hill. Jennifer lived in Colville Houses just off Talbot Road and attended Colville School in the 1950s and early '60s before going to Ladbroke School in Lancaster Road:

I used to live in Colville Houses in a flat with my parents. My parents had moved from Wales in search of work and they found themselves in Notting Hill. Our landlord was Peter Rachman, a name that everyone in the area knew. The flat was of course basic and the rent extortionate but that was the norm at the time because it was before the 1957 rent act. That of course meant that the landlords could charge what they liked and to get accommodation the immigrant population were forced into multiple occupation, very often several to a single room. Even though it was hard times I have some fond memories, like the time my Dad was watching the rugby on the old black and white TV. The backyard backed onto the backyard of the houses in Clydesdale Road. Anyway, during the match we noticed that someone had climbed onto the dividing wall between our yard and the adjacent house in Clydesdale Road. To our amazement it was Tom Jones – he was living in a bedsit and didn't have a telly but, being Welsh, loved the rugby. The ironic thing was, here was someone that had a record at the top of the charts but had to watch the rugby on our telly from his garden wall.

As I said our landlord was Rachman and his rent collector was Michael de Freitas – he always had an Alsatian dog with him. I remember that one of the flats upstairs was occupied by a young woman. She used to have a lot of male visitors at all hours. I was a bit young and didn't understand what was going on but my Dad and a young man from another flat knew and didn't

Jennifer Williams (née Sollis) in 2005.

appreciate the young prostitute carrying on business in a our house. They brought up the situation with Michael de Freitas and within a day or so she was out, not just on the street but moved to another house owned by Rachman, probably so that they could keep an eye on her so to speak – prostitution was one of his sidelines after all.

Someone else I came across when I was young was also to become famous for an even more unpleasant reason – the person was the multi murderer Christie. I remember him working part time in the Royalty Cinema in Ladbroke Grove. It's weird thinking about being in a dark cinema with someone that had murdered people.

Our doctor was Dr Oddess, an Austrian Jew whose surgery was in the road we lived in. He was also Christie's doctor and had to give evidence at the Old Bailey in his trial.

One of the places I really look back on fondly was the baths in Lancaster Road. There was [sic] two different pools with changing cubicles around the edge. They had a stable-type door with a striped canvas curtain above. I think the girls' cubicles were one side and the boys' the other and after swimming there was a canteen where you could buy a slice of bread and jam or bread and dripping for one old penny. These baths were true baths in every sense – in the 1950s and '60s most houses and flats didn't have baths or even hot running water, so the public baths were an essential public amenity – but it wasn't just baths, there were washhouses as well, because of course no one had a washing machine then.

Not all my memories are good, one somewhat unpleasant time was the Oswald Mosley period. Mosley did a lot of public speaking in the area and I remember my Dad taking me along to one of his open-air meetings on the corner of Clydesdale Road and Talbot Road. I was amazed

at the hateful way he was speaking about the coloured people. I asked my Dad why we had gone to the meeting and he said 'it's important to keep your friends close but your enemies closer'. It was shortly after this that he and other local people set up the Powis and Colville Housing Association. Its aim was to bring together immigrants and Londoners and to promote racial harmony. The association raised funds by holding jumble sales. We posted notices and went round with a handcart, borrowed from the barrow boys in Portobello Road, and collected stuff to sell – the local people were incredibly generous. At Christmas time the volunteers would go carol singing, accompanied by recorder players at Notting Hill tube station. We were joined one time by a relatively famous singing duo, I think they were called Joy and Jennifer. The money raised was used to buy goods for Christmas hampers which were distributed to local pensioners, all the produce was bought from the Welsh dairy in Talbot Road so the money was spent in the locality.

In an effort to clean up the locality the Association also helped to get prostitutes out of our area – many of course were working for Rachman and he simply re-housed them in different roads in the area. Rachman and De Freitas seemed to know everything that was going on within the association and it turned out that someone in their pay was on the committee of the association – he was confronted and never came back.

I loved school. I remember the school plays, there was one we did – The Pied Piper of Hamelin. I remember the teachers. We had a Scottish teacher called Miss Black. She would give us Scottish country-dancing lessons – the girls enjoyed it but the boys were not so enthusiastic. Then there was Mr Bromley. He was a good teacher who had an old slipper that he would use for corporal punishment. I remember once playing kiss chase with some boys and I got caught by one who tried to kiss me but I was having none of it, so he punched me. Mr Bromley saw the boy and invited me to dole out the punishment – I did it but not too hard because I knew the boy, and not Mr Bromley, would be in the playground the following day.

Of course as a child at Colville one of the most important things we had to do on the way home was to visit the sweet shop. It was Nichols on Portobello Road. The shop was run by a lovely couple, Mr Nichols looked after the ice-cream and drinks and things, oh and the wonderful frozen Jubblys [the frozen orange drink in a triangular carton]. Mr Nichols always wore a brown overall. His wife looked after the left-hand side of the shop, this was the Aladdin's cave part of the shop because it was where they sold all the 'penny sweets'. Both of them had the patience of saints, I can tell you I took ages to spend my odd few pence sweet money. Lucky bags were particularly popular with the schoolchildren but I didn't care for them.

I remember one Christmas, it was 1960 I was still at Colville but the new school in Holland Park had opened. They held a party and all the kids had to come along with a friend of a different race, so a coloured pupil had to invite

Christine Blakelock and Jennifer Sollis at Colville Houses in 1955.

a white friend and vice versa. I was invited by a girl called Gwendolyn White. The idea was to promote racial harmony, bearing in mind the Notting Hill race riots had only been about 18 months earlier. There were famous guests there too, there was musicians Cleo Laine and John Dankworth and clergyman Trevor Huddlestone, who had spent many years fighting against racial discrimination and apartheid. They really were fantastic times, even if we had little and making ends meet was difficult for everyone. I have to say I cherish all the memories.

Gill Brett was a regular visitor to the area, which makes her different from most of the other contributors and subjects in this section of this book. Gill didn't actually live in Notting Hill, but as a student in the early 1960s she spent some time in the area and has some vivid and lasting memories of Notting Hill. Gill takes up her story:

I came to Notting Hill in September 1962 to start my training to be a physiotherapist. The training took place in one of the fabulous Victorian buildings in Chepstow Villas. It was then a college run by the Tottenham Group Hospital Management Committee. I was only there for just over three years and I would travel up on a daily basis from Epsom where I lived with my mother. The college may have been No. 50 but my memory isn't that good – it was located on the northern side of the road and was only a few yards from Portobello Road, a particularly lively part of London in the swinging 1960s. The building was pretty much original when I was there except that the large rooms were equipped with desks and other equipment, there was a basement that was used as a student changing-room and cloakroom. The principal's office was located on the ground floor with the incumbent being a Scottish lady, Miss Jean Farquharson. She reminded me very much of Hattie Jacques who used to play the part of Matron in the carry on films. She was, however, a no-nonsense lady that had all of the students in awe.

Initially I was there for four days a week learning anatomy and physiology, but as time went on we spent more time at Paddington General getting more practical experience.

I remember going for lunch in a small café in Portobello Road which was run by a Greek gentleman and his wife. They used to sell delicious thick pork sausages with chips and lashings of baked beans, you know typical student food but cheap, very cheap. During the 1960s frothy coffee was all the rage and we would go to another little café on Notting Hill Gate near the tube station for this fashionable refreshment. There must have been a ballet school nearby because it was also frequented by ballet students.

I remember another student rented and later purchased a basement flat in the Westbourne Grove area. She paid very little at the time for the property but I suspect its worth a small fortune now and she still lives there. I think that after several years as a practising physio she gave it up to help a friend run his antique shop – very Notting Hill!

Gill had a very happy time in Notting Hill and has found, as do most visitors, that something of the area has rubbed off on her. She clearly enjoyed and gained from her connections with the Royal Borough.

The last remaining Victorian residential building in Clydesdale Road. This was once a terrace that ran from Westbourne Park Road to Talbot Road.

Looking towards Kensington Park Road from Chepstow Villas.

Left: *The almost-white stone façade of the Church of St John the Evangelist.*

Below: *A sketch of the Church of St John the Evangelist.* (REDRAWN BY M. WILKINSON)

Chapter 8

The Estates of Notting Hill

The estates of Notting Hill have been a feature that has persisted from the onset of the residential development of the area. We can look at the present-day maps and discern the vague outlines of the great products of early developers and speculators. Many of these grand developments were destined to create the style and personality of the area and would stand the test of time through world wars, boom and bust and even, in many cases, modern developers' ambitions.

Some of the land used for the 'new' estates became available because of the downfall of the Hippodrome in the mid-1800s. Other speculators probably felt that the spread of urban development would soon catch up with the farm and meadow lands to the west of the metropolis, and how right they turned out to be.

The story begins with the farms and smallholdings on the manor of the De Vere family. The Middlesex woods were cleared, and for centuries the land was used for arable farming. The farms of Notting Barns and Portobello were destined to be swallowed up by urban development, although their immediate surroundings remained a peaceful oasis in the hands of the religious orders that became their owners, for some years anyway.

It is difficult to define what the estates were, or indeed to always separate one from its neighbour – a good reason for this is that much of the design work was undertaken by the same architects. This was almost unprecedented co-operation and it was this very co-operation that allowed the virtually seamless linking of various estates and projects in terms of roadways and communications. We have a more defined image of the estates, as they have become the council-housing projects, such as Lancaster West or Henry Dickens court – housing developments that sprang up after the war to replace housing lost to German bombing, or as a result of slum clearance during the 1960s and '70s.

Some of the early estates were the dreams of the wealthy men of the Victorian age, in a time of boom when the building industry was creating much of the rapidly expanding capital. By the late 1830s the west of London had only reached as far as Kensington Gardens, and was surrounded by open country occupied by clusters of houses, farms and small outcrops of industry such as the brickfield. Parts of Chelsea and Kensington were still given over to market gardens and animal keeping, especially pigs which were fed on the discarded food waste of the affluent parts of adjoining boroughs.

Further west, settlements were scattered around main roads or other geographic features such as crossroads, wells or farms – indeed, as with Notting Hill or Portobello, the names of these farms or their owners can be seen on present-day maps, reflected in districts, estates, roads or local features.

The failure of the Hippodrome left Mr Whyte in a position that required the racecourse be broken up, with the eastern end being the first piece to go. The estate landlord was Mr J.W. Ladbroke who saw fit to let the land to a Mr Connop. Building work had started even before the racecourse was finally closed, with property being erected in what is now Kensington Park Road. Some of the dwellings were so well designed and beautiful that the plans were exhibited at the Royal Academy. The market for such large houses in an area considered at the time to be 'so far from London' left Mr Connop insolvent with debts of between £60,000 and £70,000 – a vast amount in the 1840s, bearing in mind that a reasonable house in the area could be purchased for less than £200.

The Mr Ladbroke took over the project and saw it through to conclusion, with the appointment of architect Mr Allom. The project became known as the Kensington Park estate and would be topped with a magnificent church at its highest point. The church was finished in the 1850s and was named St John the Evangelist. It stood surrounded by open land and gained the nickname St John's in the Hayfields. It was the best-situated and designed church in the parish and remains a delightful sight.

The estate boasted a wide tree-lined boulevard which is now known a Ladbroke Grove, just one legacy of the gentleman whose vision finally gave us some of the most beautiful buildings in this part of North Kensington. Mr Ladbroke's name is destined to be a feature of the area for a long time to come.

The beautiful Stanley Gardens part of the Ladbroke estate.

Above left: *A plaque describing St James's Gardens.*

Above: *St James Norland, another church in the area originally designed to have a spire on top of the tower. A lack of funds curtailed its building along with several houses on the northern side of the square.*

Left: *The residential properties in St James's Square.*

Below: *Looking like a tree-lined boulevard in the suburbs of Paris, this is Chepstow Villas.*

The outstanding Royal Crescent on the edge of Norland Town, a particularly fine piece of architecture.

Portland Road at the junction of Hippodrome Place, almost the only reminder of its racing past.

The church of St John the Evangelist was consecrated in January 1845, six months earlier than its sister church St James's Norland, another district destined to change from rural town to developed estate and later slum district. Norland Town is a name that has persisted over many years and indeed can still be heard in 2006. Norland abutted Shepherd's Bush where the M41 now meets the Uxbridge Road, and it was the building of this link to the Westway extension (A41(M)) that finally removed the majority of Norland Road.

Norland was an area that included many of the poorest inhabitants of Notting Dale, but ironically also boasts a fabulous development called the Royal Crescent and hosted an outdoor market that in its day rivalled Portobello Road. It is home to St Anns Villas, groups of substantial buildings with a long rollercoaster history. But its most notorious set of thoroughfares are the roads that made up the Potteries. These roads were made up of slums, huts, cabins and even old caravans, which created a scene only found in the very poorest parts of the realm. There were a huge number of alehouses with almost every road having one, and it was this fact, along with the low price of gin, that led to high levels of drunkenness. Over the next couple of decades the Church was represented by almost all branches of Christian belief – everything from the Salvation Army with their large 'Citadel', to the Wesleyans with their attractive chapels, to the Roman Catholic St Francis of Assisi Church and School, and, as mentioned at the beginning of this paragraph, the Church of St James. It is interesting to note that, as with All Saints Church, St James's was also originally designed with a spire atop of its tower, but unfortunately, due to a lack of funds, this was never built. But even unfinished the church does not look out of proportion. It is a beautiful church that can be seen at its best when approached from Addison Avenue.

It was the 1850s when the area was really changing out of all recognition with building increasing.

The Potteries and brickfields were all but worked out and the Hippodrome had closed, which meant land was available for development. Initially the building of large detached and paired villas was the order of the day. However, the buying public were not convinced that the area was right for this type of middle-class property and plans were changed. The architects, monied men and purchasers demanded a different type of property – small terraced cottages for the artisans that were moving into the area, three and four-storied terraces to be used as tenements for the poorer types and even premises for businesses and schools.

During the 1860s there was an influx of the very poor and those displaced from other London areas. It was a time when building work was changing many parts of the capital and the slum clearance meant that people needed cheap accommodation – Norland, or Notting Dale as it was becoming known, could fulfil their needs. Many of the properties were let out on a floor or room basis and many of the larger houses in the former Potteries became common boarding-houses. The influx of poor people was turning the area from one type of slum to another, with prostitutes, thieves, footpads and drunks roaming the streets of the Dale.

Norland also became a shopping area with Saturday and Sunday markets being held in the roads. These markets were rag markets, selling secondhand clothes, etc, and were held in Clarendon Road, Bangor Road, Crescent Street and Sirdar Road, the inhabitants of which were heavily biased toward the totting trade which meant a constant supply of old shoes, clothes and other pre-owned goods. Norland Road market leant more towards other goods such as fruit and vegetables, and other food-stuff, and also had a good selection of shops lining the road. Provisions were purchased on a daily basis, as there were no hygienic food storage facilities and refrigerators were not in existence. Norland and Shepherd's Bush market, as it was originally known,

The Portland Road area has become a fashionable village-like area – the housing is renovated and smart.

Left: *Latimer School dwarfed by the high-rise flats of the area.*

Below left: *Talbot Road, to the front of All Saints Church, is now closed to traffic and is much calmer.*

Below: *Queensdale Road in the heart of Norland Town.*

was in business through to the mid-twentieth century. At the time of the market's conception Uxbridge Road in adjacent Shepherd's Bush was not a commercial area and was lined with residential properties, giving the market a ready supply of customers. Shepherd's Bush now has its own market between Uxbridge Road and Goldhawk Road, adjacent to the Hammersmith and City Line railway, with shops incorporated into the arches of the elevated track.

The reason for the upsurge and indeed later demise of the Sunday market is also interesting. In the early years workers were not paid until Saturday evening, the end of the working week – clearly the employers did not trust the employees to turn up for work if they were paid in advance. Getting paid on a Saturday meant two things; firstly, Saturday evening was a good time to go drinking but not the time for shopping, therefore the non-working day of Sunday became the day the wives would search the markets for cheap goods to be bought with the now alcoholically-depleted wage packet. It was early Sunday morning that the 'rag fair' was held, when local people would push barrows, or even old prams, into Crescent Street and set up stalls selling anything they could get hold of, usually by 'totting' during the week.

This was mainly a totting area, but there was also a lot of employment within the transport industry. There were lots of stables and workshops with many of the locals employed by the General Omnibus Company as stablemen, car men or cab washers. The horse-drawn buses were an important means of transport, along with the trains – both of which would carry passengers to and from work in the capital. Another major trade in the area was laundry – at times it must have seemed that every woman in the district was employed as a laundry worker. It was such an industry that a man was considered to be lucky to marry 'a good ironing woman'.

One feature of the Potteries and Norland estate was the Salvation Army Citadel, which was originally built in 1859 as the Norland chapel at the junction of Queensdale Road and Norland Road. It was the new home for the Baptist congregation under Revd Stent, who moved there from the old building adjacent to Shepherd's Bush. After using the chapel for less than 20 years the building was taken over by the Christian Mission under Revd Booth. The Christian Mission are better known as the Salvation Army and the chapel was renamed as Norland Castle. The building was seriously damaged by fire in the 1960s but by that time the Salvation Army had vacated the premises and fortunately it was empty. The fire was captured on camera by a young member of the Worley family, a well-known local dynasty of traders and totters who have been in the area for generations. The picture made the front page of the *West London Observer* on Thursday 10 September 1964.

Another 'estate' with quite a history is the Latymer area, which has close links with the Potteries

and Norland, as it was here that the Piggeries were located. It was almost a village on its own, separated for many years by open fields and totally inadequate and badly-maintained roads and tracks. Indeed on one occasion the poor condition of one particular road cost the life of Frances Dowlin. It was the morning of 23 January 1860 when her body was found lying in the middle of Latimer Road, not a victim of robbers but of the atrocious condition of the road itself. Returning home at around 11pm she missed the 'crossing point' and fell into a miry pit. Her cries for help were heard, but in this time of drunken street brawls they went unheeded – who would rise from their bed just to witness another drunk falling around?

In Florence Gladstone's book *Notting Hill in Days Gone By*, she describes the location of the mission hall, built in 1863:

... the hall with one attached classroom stands in the midst of a primeval swamp blossoming with broken bottles, pot and pans with the only means of approach being a narrow track bordered by white posts a necessary precaution on winter evenings.

It appears that this area was forgotten by most bodies of authority. The area was considered to be an outlying area belonging to the parish of St Stephen's in Shepherd's Bush. By 1864 it was obvious that the religious authorities needed to make these outlying areas into a new ecclesiastical district.

Along with the developing estate of Norland James Whitchurch wanted to emulate the blossoming Ladbroke estate. Mr Whitchurch was a property developer from Southampton. He purchased 49 acres of former farm land and built houses in Walmer, Bramley and Lancaster Roads, but it was in Silchester Road that he really tried to bring to fruition his dreams of an estate of large, light and airy properties set in their own gardens. His plans were never to be fully realised, as the viaduct of the Hammersmith and City railway cut across his part-finished street. Clearly the type of resident he wished to attract would not want to invest in a residence in such close proximity to this particular amenity. Again, as with other areas, plans changed and smaller terraced properties were built. However, even the middle classes were not impressed by the noise, smell and dirt thrown up by the railway, and inevitably these properties ended up as tenements and lodging-houses. It was also in this area that one of the most used, and indeed loved, local amenities in the Dale was located, on the junction of Silchester and Lancaster Road – the Kensington Baths and washhouse which opened in 1888 and closed in the 1970s.

In the Latimer area during the 1970s another means of transport cut a community in half – the A41(M) Westway extension carved its way through the Latimer, Silchester and Frestonia part of the

Above: *Looking regal, the fine Victorian edifices of Colville Terrace.*

Right: *Looking up Talbot Road towards All Saints Church.*

Below: *Family homes in Bonchurch Road. In the 1960s these houses would have been used as multiple-occupancy dwellings.*

estate, and in the subsequent clearance many of the nineteenth-century tenements were lost, but not without a fight.

It was in this atmosphere that the Independent State of Frestonia was born – not exactly an estate itself, but it was the efforts of the Frestonians that forced the authorities to abandon their plans to use the newly available land for industrial purposes. In the aftermath of, and as a direct result of the Frestonia period, a new estate was eventually born – an estate of high- and low-rise dwellings with an emphasis on community. These estates had their teething problems. Many of the stairwells and walkways were dimly lit and became a haven for muggers and drug dealers. However, it was an estate with a community spirit and the old Frestonians and new residents were not to be easily beaten – they stuck together and eventually overcame the problems of modern estate dwelling.

In the heart of Notting Dale nestles yet another estate, not as modern as the Lancaster West and definitely not as old as either the Norland or Ladbroke estates, but it was probably one of the first modern estates of flats planned for North Kensington. Henry Dickens Court is located in the heart of the Potteries and was built as part of an early slum-clearance programme planned in the mid-1930s and completed in the early '50s. Bangor and Crescent Street had been the subject of a compulsory-purchase order by Kensington Borough Council before the war. It was to be a full-scale rehousing programme but the onset of the Second World War meant the building of Henry Dickens Court had to wait. Demolition of the roads finally started in 1947 and the new flats were completed in 1952, but it was to late for many of the original residents of this run-down set of streets because by now they had moved away from Notting Dale. The fact that the community had broken up because of delays did not mean that there wasn't a ready-made supply of potential residents – redevelopment schemes in other areas meant that, as in the 1800s, affordable accommodation was at a premium. By January 1955 Henry Dickens Court was fully occupied and a community was in the process of developing. It is a fact that the new residents were by and large Notting Dale folk, and as such knew how to create a real community.

When the great estates such as Ladbroke and Norland were planned one thing appeared obligatory, and that was a fine church to tend to the religious needs of the residents. The churches were designed as a focal point, built at the highest or most central point of the community – All Saints Church is no exception. It is probably the most distinctive church for miles around, partly because of its unfinished appearance and partly because of where it is located. It has been described as 'probably the most beautiful thing in the whole of North Kensington when seen at sunset against the western sky.' The land around was not

always so inviting. It became known for some time as 'All Sinners in the mud' or 'Walkers Folly' after Revd Dr Walker, who was the owner of the church and more land in its vicinity. Dr Walker had purchased 55 acres of land from Mary Anne and Georgina Charlotte Talbot and had proceeded to build what he had intended to be 'a new town'. It was unfortunate that Dr Walker had left himself somewhat financially overstretched, mainly due to his ambitious plans for his new town and the considerable amount of building he had already undertaken. Dr Walker was originally from North Cornwall and had come to London to invest half a million sterling in property. What he created was a huge amount of unfinished dwellings too far from central London and on the wrong side of the area. Dr Walker was left almost ruined and had to abandon many of his plans, including those of his new town around the Church of All Saints. The land opposite the church and as far as Lonsdale, Ledbury and Portobello Roads was sold to a Messers Tibbetts to be used as a brickfield. The church was left unfinished and surrounded by a muddy field which was often inhabited by gypsies, and many of his grand dwellings closer to the Potteries were left unfinished for many years.

The Tibbetts were not the types to let their investments tick over and in time they were credited with building Colville and Powis Squares, and indeed most of the residential roads which eventually covered the All Saints fields.

At the northern end of Portobello Road and Golborne Road new estates have sprung up. It was this area which was first to be almost cut off by the A40(M) Westway extension. The area is surrounded by barriers – the railway bounds the north and east, as does the canal, the south is bounded by the A40(M) and to the west is Ladbroke Grove, probably the busiest thoroughfare in the locality. Little wonder then that this end of Portobello Road seems different to the rest of the area – it is an area that has become a haven for the Spanish and Portuguese communities of North Kensington. Estates run almost unhindered from Aklam Road to the Harrow Road and are only stopped by the physical barriers of main roads like Ladbroke Grove and the canal. At the north-eastern end of Golborne Road stands the tallest building in the area. Trellick Tower is a tower block which was built during the slum clearance years of the early 1970s. It stands head and shoulders above everything else in the area, and probably in the whole of Kensington. Even as it ages, and you become accustomed to its vastness and '70s looks, I personally find it hard to find anything attractive about this building – it has been said that this listed building's moment of glory will be its demolition.

On the other side of Ladbroke Grove there is another estate which is on the site of the old Sunbeam works. It stretches as far as Little Wormwood Scrubs and is bordered again by the railway to the north and to the south it goes almost as far as the A40(M). This is a different type of estate, for although it was originally in the main a council-estate, the housing is generally made up of two-storey red-brick terraced houses. The estate has grown up over many years and has surrounded parks, hospitals and even monasteries, and it is this growth that makes it difficult to actually put a boundary on the estate. In loose terms I have lumped it together with Delgarno (which includes low-level flats) and much of the old Sunbeam Talbot works. Along St Marks Roads, Cambridge Gardens and Exmoor Street there are also medium-sized Victorian terraces, but even these seem to mingle with smaller housing in the locality.

What makes it difficult to separate the estates, if indeed they are estates, is the diversity of buildings that make them up. There is everything from towering blocks of flats to small cottage-type terraced housing. There are the old Victorian villas, as seen in the likes of the Ladbroke estate, and the now-lost prefabricated buildings that were put up on a temporary basis after the war – temporary dwellings that in many cases lasted 40 years. It is this mix of buildings that makes up the estates of North Kensington, but their main ingredient was and is the people that live there. The gypsy camps of the Potteries and Piggeries may have been seasonal, and their dwellings caravans, but the people that came every year eventually stayed, and in staying started a community. The same can be said of the laundry workers or the manual workers of the brickfields or pottery works, and in more recent years the West Indian community. The estates are not only buildings – they are the people that populate them.

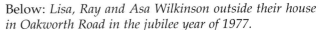
Left: *The answer to the loss of housing during German bombing in the Second World War – the prefab. This was supposed to be temporary housing. However, many were still occupied 40 years later.*

Below: *Lisa, Ray and Asa Wilkinson outside their house in Oakworth Road in the jubilee year of 1977.*

Chapter 9

Boats, Trains and Buses

The transport systems in and around Notting Hill have developed as the population moved in, businesses grew up, demand increased and technology and needs changed. The Paddington branch of the Grand Junction Canal, which was opened in 1801, cuts across the northern side of the borough and was an important artery into the centre of London. It brought goods and raw materials in from the industrial heartland of Birmingham and the Midlands and transported finished goods into London. Bricks and building materials from the Notting Hill Potteries were a major part of the cargo which was essential for the expanding residential districts that were growing up all over and around Victorian London. Household waste was a byproduct of this residential expansion, so the barges brought the waste back out to the dumps on the outskirts of the capital.

The docks on the canal were served by horse-drawn barges in the years before mechanically powered barges, and the bridal path can still be found running along the side of the canal. When tunnels or steep cuttings where encountered the horses would be unhitched and walked past the obstruction – at this point the bargees would have to 'leg it'. The term 'leg it' refers to a method of propelling the barge along a tunnel – the bargee lay on his back and walked along the side wall of the tunnel, thus moving the barge along.

Although the heyday of the canal had passed by the turn of the century barges could still be seen carrying cargoes until the mid-twentieth century, although the cargo consisted of sightseeing parties and holiday-makers – a new breed of narrow-boat enthusiast had started to use the network for pleasure. As a child my family would catch a water bus at Little Venice, which is near Maida Vale, and cruise sedately through Regent's Park to London Zoo. The canal is not ready to lay to waste, and a new initiative launched in 2005 saw a stretch in the Golborne area being cleaned up and the towpath renovated, allowing local residents to make use of it for walks and leisure activities.

The Grand Junction Canal was joined in the area by a second canal in 1826 – the Kensington Canal, which roughly followed the western boundary of the area. It was to be a short-lived venture and by 1836 was sold to the West London Railway and was drained. The new railway was also short-lived in its first incarnation, as discussed later in this chapter.

Notting Hill was also served well by trains with Brunel's Great Western Railway entering the borough close to, and following, the canal to Paddington.

Paddington Station is one of Brunel's finest edifices – constructed of cast iron and glass it boasts huge sweeping arches across the platforms.

Isambard Kingdom Brunel was a resident of Kensington and Chelsea, living at 98 Cheyne Walk, as did his father Sir Marc Isambard Brunel.

I remember as a child going to the station prior to Paddington (Royal Oak) to watch the steam trains going on their journeys. I would often stand on the road bridge over the track and watch the smoke rise – a wonderful experience. The smell now is slightly different, being of diesel and sparking electric pick ups, but still the line through the borough of Kensington and Chelsea is a masterpiece, carrying passengers down to Bristol and beyond. The line passes the old GWR capital, Swindon, and on to the Box tunnel near Bath, which hid the wartime cabinet and control bunker, then it's on to Bath, Bristol, the west coast and Wales.

During the 1960s British Rail were changing their rolling stock, from steam to diesel and electric. Many of the steam locos were destined for the scrapyards but some examples ended up on preserved lines or in museums. Early one Sunday morning in the mid-1960s, a large steam loco had been taken off the tracks at Westbourne Park Station and loaded onto a low-loader, ready to make the rest of its journey by road. The load had made its way successfully as far as the junction of All Saints Road and Westbourne Park Road, but for some time that was as far as it was going. The length of the vehicle was such that it got halfway round the junction and had got stuck, and no amount of manoeuvring could get it round. It was stuck like this for hours, and only continued its journey after a heavy-lifting gear was brought in to sort the problem out.

The Grand Junction Canal with the Kensal Green Cemetery on the right and the Western Gas Company's gasometers on the left.

97

Above: *Looking across the lines of the Great West Railway with the tower of St Charles Hospital opposite.*

Left: *The lines of the GWR at the site of the Ladbroke Grove rail disaster.*

Below: *Ladbroke Grove Station, which is served by the Hammersmith and City Line.*

That was not the end of the All Saints Road train – the following day the water main under the spot were the train came to a rest gave in and burst, sending a fountain of water in the air as high as my bedroom window above the Co-op hall, which was above the Co-op shop, making the fountain at least 35 feet in height.

In more recent years the railway and Ladbroke Grove have made the headlines for all the wrong reasons. On 5 October 1999 a passenger train passed a red signal at Ladbroke Grove in West London and collided with a high-speed train. A total of 31 people died and over 400 others were injured. As a result of the crash and a similar accident at Southall the Health and Safety Executive made 295 safety-related recommendations and initiated a separate enquiry into the need and use of Train Protection and Warning Systems (TPWS), along with measures to prevent trains passing red signals. The enquiry report was published in 2000 with a further 39 recommendations. Thames Trains were charged with offences under the Health and Safety at Work Act, relating specifically to training issues – the company pleaded guilty and received a fine of £2 million, a record penalty for a health-and-safety-related offence.

The GWR wasn't the only train service in Notting Hill. Although short-lived as a passenger service, the West London Railway warrants a mention. The WLR linked Willesden Junction with Clapham Junction via Latimer Road and Kensington Olympia, with parts being opened as early as 1840. In 1844 the WLR started operating a passenger service, but this was not a success and lasted less than a year. The rail service was doomed to be a failure and early lampooning in *Punch* led to its nickname 'Punch's Railway'. By 1845 the WLR was purely a freight operation.

Yet another, and an even earlier service, just coming into the area, was between Paddington and Westbourne Park, and was opened in 1838 by the Great Western Railway.

In 1864 a new train service was born. The Hammersmith and City Railway (H&CR), as it was known, ran through Notting Hill from Latimer Road, Notting Hill Station (now Ladbroke Grove) and Westbourne Park and incorporated the oldest underground line in the world, which runs between Paddington and Farringdon. By 1867 the Metropolitan Railway purchased a share of the H&CR from GWR and the line soon became the Metropolitan, a name that in one form or another remained until 1990 when the name Hammersmith and City Line was revived and the service separated from the Metropolitan line services.

Some statistics worth putting down in print are that the H&CL is nine miles long and services 19 stations along its route. It carries an annual total of 45 million passengers and requires 17 trains of six cars for a full peak-time service.

In 1998 the government announced that the underground would be run by a Public Private Partnership (PPP) with Metronet SSL contracted to upgrade, renew and maintain the Hammersmith and City Line.

Buses are an essential part of life in the area, giving access to central London and further afield to the outlying suburbs. The 'big red buses' have been a feature of roads like Westbourne Park Road, Ladbroke Grove and Westbourne Grove for decades. In earlier incarnations the buses would have been horse-drawn with open tops, and indeed one bus company, the General Omnibus Company, had a large facility in the area located adjacent to Avondale Park. Later on trolley buses that had overhead electric pick ups would have been seen, but whatever type we remember fondly, their importance and value to the community is not in question.

As an 11-year-old boy I was enrolled in a new school in Shepherd's Bush – until that point I had attended Colville Junior Mixed School in nearby Lonsdale Road. That journey was a 15 minute walk away – a walk that I had made without adult assistance from the age of about six or seven. I was now

The next station up the line from Ladbroke Grove is Westbourne Park, where the Hammersmith and City line meets the GWR.

No. 7 buses in Westbourne Park Road, June 2005.

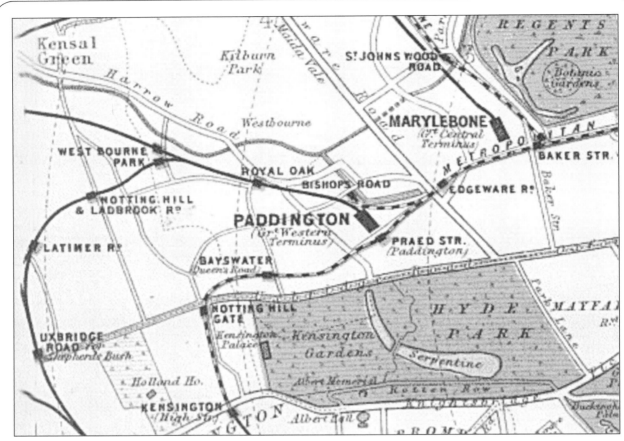

Above: *A section of the 1899 railway map, showing the GWR, Metropolitan and Hammersmith and City Line.*

Left: *The view from the A41(M) Westway extension, looking between the safety barriers up Portobello Road.*

Below: *Looking down Ladbroke Grove towards the Westway and Ladbroke Grove underground station.*

about to make a quantum leap in three respects: firstly I was to go to a new school with new teachers, a massively daunting task for an 11 year old; secondly I was going out of my immediate neighbourhood, again somewhat daunting for a boy that new virtually every nook and cranny of W11; and thirdly, the journey on the No. 7 bus – and all without being late or losing the return bus fare during the school day. After the first few days all the worries were forgotten and the journey on the big red Routemaster bus became an enjoyable part of my school years. I can still remember the sound of the ticket machine and the bell, one ring to stop the bus at a request stop and two from the conductor to tell the driver to drive on. The cost for this 20 minute bus journey was a 2d. half – the half refers to half fare for a child under 14 (it was two pence in pre-decimal coinage and that equates to less than one new penny). During school holidays we would buy a 'red rover' ticket for about half a crown (two shillings and sixpence or 12½ new pence) which gave us the entire London Transport network for a day. My mates (Mark Rawley, Chris Thompson or Frank Lamb) and I would go all over London getting back home at about dusk – not bad for 11 and 12 year olds.

The London bus network is the largest in the world in 2006 and employs in excess of 22,000 drivers, but it is still a disappointment for many of the transport purists that the days of the 'clippie' (conductor) are virtually over. It is a result of the phasing out of the old London Transport designed 'AEC Routemaster' buses, the last of the open-platform buses which are being replaced by fully enclosed, one-man-operated vehicles. However, in October 2005 Transport for London announced what it calls 'Heritage Routes', which will continue to operate a number of Routemasters. Fortunately, one of those routes is No. 15, running from Kensington Albert Hall to Aldwych, with the other being the No. 9 from Hammersmith.

The AEC Routemaster is a part of West London's history in its own right, as they were built at the AEC works in Southall and Park Royal with help from the London Transport works at Chiswick right up to the end of production in 1968. During the ten years of production of the Associated Equipment Company's Routemaster bus, almost 3,000 examples were built. AEC built buses for London Transport between 1912 and 1979.

As a child during the 1950s and '60s I remember the road traffic going from one or two cars a minute, and very little roadside parking, to gridlock, even on the side roads that became rat runs for drivers trying to avoid the traffic congestion of a modern metropolis. By the middle of the 1960s a project was underway to take the M41 Westway extension through the borough and on to the centre of London, whilst in the process taking large amounts of traffic off the overcrowded city streets of Kensington. When the road was built large areas of North Kensington became a building site – some 700 houses were demolished and streets were cut in two. The A40(M) is an elevated motorway constructed on giant concrete pylons and was, at the time, the largest concrete structure in England.

The Westway speeds commuters to and from the heart of London over the heads of a community which it has divided in two – 47,000 cars a day have brought a constant, intrusive and unwanted barrage of noise and light pollution to this deprived part of London. Unfortunately, the volume of vehicles on the area's streets has still increased to intolerable levels and parking is virtually impossible for all but the most determined, but I guess that's progress for you.

The battle for the Westway was fought hard by local residents from Dale and Hill – a battle that is still being fought, not now for housing because hopefully that battle is under control, but a battle for amenities, both social and civil.

A No. 7 AEC Routemaster of First London, pictured in 2003.

Left: *No. 60 Elgin Crescent, the former home of Jawaharlal (Pandit) Nehru.*

Below: *The Chepstow Villas home of Lajos (Louis) Kossuth.*

Chapter 10
Famous and Infamous

Notting Hill has had more than its fair share of famous and infamous residents. Some we remember, some we know, some we don't and some we are not aware that we know, but many are interesting and are worthy a mention in any community history book. Whilst walking around the borough look out for the blue plaques on buildings – you may be surprised at who has lived in the houses in your road. However, not all the famous and infamous have plaques.

You may not know the name John Reginald Haliday Christie but you will probably know his former address, 10 Rillington Place, from the film of the same name. Christie was the most notorious murderer in Notting Hill. Originally from Yorkshire, Christie had deserted his wife after being sacked from several jobs and serving time in prison for theft of postal orders. He came to London but was soon in trouble with the law again, serving three further terms in prison. Following separation for some ten years, his wife joined him in London, which was to prove a fatal mistake on her part. Incredible as it may seem, Christie managed to become a wartime reserve policeman serving at Harrow Road police station and even earning himself a commendation. Christie's seven victims were all women (excluding the Evans' daughter, whom he never admitted killing). However, he was responsible for the death of one male – his neighbour Timothy Evans, who was hanged for the murder of his wife and child. At his trial Christie gave crucial evidence, but it was, as we now know, Christie who was responsible for their murders.

Christie eventually became mentally unstable and left his ground-floor flat, but the new tenant soon discovered the truth about the 'house of horror' in Rillington Place. Christie had gone on the run, although he remained in and around London, but his freedom was to be short-lived as he was quickly spotted by an alert PC near the Star and Garter public house in Putney. He was arrested, charged and stood trial in court number one at the Old Bailey, which was ironically the same court in which he had given evidence against Evans.

In British Law at that time he had to be tried for one murder at a time, so he was tried and found guilty of the murder of his wife on 22 June and was hanged in 1953.

It was public concern about the miscarriage of justice and subsequent execution of Evans that mobilised public concern over the death penalty, which was finally abolished in 1965.

Timothy Evans was given a posthumous free pardon in 1966 and was re-buried with his wife and daughter in North London. No. 10 Rillington Place was demolished in the 1970s when the Westway extension was built – it stood approximately where Bartle Street and Rushton Mews are in 2006.

It's not every day that someone comes along whose name is entered into the Oxford English Dictionary, but one such person was Peter Rachman. Rachmanism is defined in the dictionary as 'the exploitation or intimidation of tenants by unscrupulous landlords'. Peter, or to give him his correct name Perec Rachman, was a Polish refugee who came to England during the Second World War. He started work in neighbouring Shepherd's Bush and soon came to the conclusion that the postwar housing shortage would have its advantages for an unscrupulous businessman. To start off his empire he bought up a number of run-down properties in the Paddington and Notting Hill areas with money borrowed from a building society. Unfortunately, many of these properties were cheap because they had sitting tenants, a problem Rachman would not let hinder his enthusiasm for making money.

Rachman needed to get rid of these 'unprofitable tenants' and so devised a very effective three-step method of persuading them to vacate their homes in favour of more profitable occupants: 1. Offer a small payment to leave; 2. All-night parties and loud music in adjacent flats or rooms; 3. Cut off water, electricity and gas, break locks and sanitary fittings. These acts were carried out by heavies in Rachman's employ and tenants would usually succumb to their persuasive ways and vacate the premises, or pay increased rents without further steps being required.

The more profitable tenants tended to be immigrants, mainly Afro-Caribbean or Irish families who had nowhere else to go. It was common at that time to see signs in the windows of vacant rented accommodation stating 'no blacks, no Irish, no dogs', and so these people had no alternative but to pay extortionate rents for rooms owned by Rachman, who made no racial discrimination when it came to making money.

Rachman moved to Hampstead on the profits of his property empire and was driven around in a chauffeur-driven Rolls Royce. I can vaguely remember seeing him on a few occasions. He was a man most people in the area recognised by the late 1950s.

By 1959 a special police unit was set up to investigate Rachman's businesses, which were many and included a sideline of prostitution which led to him being prosecuted on two occasions for keeping brothels. In 1960 for no apparent reason Rachman disposed of his properties but he died in 1962, a millionaire.

I will leave the reader to decide whether the next resident of W11 is famous or infamous – even though I have my own opinion I will try to write with balance on the man who was Michael de Freitas.

Michael was born in Trinidad in 1933 to a Barbadian mother and white father, with whom he had little contact – his early years were spent living with his grandmother. It was apparent from an early age that Michael would be a bit of a tearaway and he gained something of a reputation by the age of 14, at which point he was asked to leave the Catholic school he attended. He was thus put in the position of seeking early employment, but over the next few years his work record was poor and a fraud incident led him to make the decision of going to sea, and he joined a Norwegian shipping company as a galley boy. This was the opportunity he had been waiting for – his dream of travelling, especially to England, was to be realised. He later attempted to join the British merchant fleet but was not able to secure a position because of his colour. He again signed up with the Norwegians.

Michael spent time in the Tiger Bay area of Cardiff between voyages, where he became a common figure amongst the criminal fraternity. His career at sea saw him rise to Chief Petty Officer but he was itching to get to London, an ambition that would come to fruition in the mid-1950s. Notting Hill was about to meet Michael de Freitas.

Once based in London he set about getting known – he turned his hand to stealing suitcases from Heathrow airport. He was also involved in the smuggling of a young Yugoslavian girl into the UK and became known to the UK authorities. He was questioned but never charged over the incident. As for the girl, she had a lucky escape from the life of vice that Michael had planned for her.

The money Michael needed came from gambling, vice and other petty criminal activities. However, he decided to try his hand at bigger things and was recruited into a gang planning an armed robbery in Berkshire. The robbery failed but it was his actions that led to part of the legend being inflated. The leader of the gang fainted during the raid, at which point Michael calmly picked him up with a fireman's lift and carried him to the waiting getaway car – a novel start and finish to a career in the armed-robbery business.

By this time he was beginning to meet a certain type of person – with one of them being 'Peter the Pole' Rachman. Rachman decided he could use a man with the talents of de Freitas and he became one of his 'rent collectors'.

The gathering storm clouds of unrest between the black and white communities gave de Freitas yet another tool with which to add to his reputation, and

he was amongst a group of young black males who made a stand against groups of Teddy boys in Blenheim Crescent during the Notting Hill race riots. Michael de Freitas and the other black men sent the white 'Teds' scattering with the use of Molotov cocktails, machetes and iron bars. The stand had galvanised the police into action on subsequent nights and things started to quieten down. There was a feeling that the battle had started to glean results, and the police would make greater efforts to stop the racial attacks and keep the streets peaceful and safe.

Even with the atmosphere between the two communities in Notting Hill more comfortable it was still a time of racial struggle. Things were happening both in England and the US. In the US Malcolm X and his Black Power movement were in the headlines and his visit to the UK gave de Freitas the chance to meet up with the black American activist. Michael de Freitas persuaded Malcolm X to visit Notting Hill – a move that allowed him to bask in the reflected limelight of the American activist. De Freitas started to believe he was a local, if not an ethnic, leader. Soon Michael de Freitas took the name Michael X and set up a 'black house' in the area, and later formed a branch of the Afro-American Unity Organisation in the UK.

Michael de Freitas was credited with being a leading light in starting the carnival in Notting Hill, setting up the London Free School and the UK's first underground newspaper *International Times* or *IT* as it became known.

There is doubt about a lot of these claims. However, what is fact is that in 1967 he became the first person to be charged with 'inciting racial hatred' and served time in Swansea prison. By 1970 Michael Abdul Malik, as he became known, was again involved when trouble flared up at the Mangrove Café in All Saints Road, but with unrelated charges hanging over him – this time it was extortion, and the extent of his involvement is questionable. During this time the black house he set up started to fall apart as members and staff rebelled against the leadership. Michael was busy raising defence funds with money coming from people such as John Lennon and Muhammad Ali.

In early 1971 de Freitas left England for the last time and his connections with London W11 were severed. Many felt this was the best thing that could have happened for local race relations. Michael Campbell de Freitas was later charged with murder and sentenced to death. Following appeals and time on death row he faced the gallows on 16 May 1975 in Port of Spain, Trinidad.

One former resident of the borough enjoyed the Victorian splendour of No. 60 Elgin Crescent and the beauty of an official residence in India. Jawaharlal (also known as Pandit) Nehru (1889–1964) was the first Prime Minister of India.

Nehru became Indian Prime Minister in 1947, having studied law at Cambridge and became a lawyer in the Allahabad High Court. Ironically, he was greatly influenced by Ghandi and was imprisoned on several occasions by the British.

He was elected to the Indian Congress Committee in 1918 and was elected to position of Committee President in 1929. On being elected Indian Prime Minister he maintained a policy of strict neutrality during the Cold War.

Victorian splendour was something that the following resident was also used to – in fact he spent most of his working time in the splendid surroundings of Victorian music halls and in his private life at home in No. 1 St Anns Villas. Albert Chevalier was an actor, making his debut in 1877. By 1888 he reluctantly changed his discipline to reciting comic songs and monologues. His debut in the music halls came in 1891 and he soon became very successful as a 'coster comedian'. He was a favourite of royalty and the wealthy, often performing in the drawing-rooms of large London houses. In 1906 he toured the US and Canada with Yvette Guilbert, the singer and cabaret artist.

Notting Hill clearly has its fair share of foreign statesmen and the next entry again held positions of power. Lajos (Louis) Kossuth was born in 1802 in Hungary. He studied law and became a lawyer and political journalist, for which he was imprisoned between 1837 and 1840. In 1847 he became leader of the opposition and demanded an independent government for Hungary. However, it was the following year that he made his mark. The year 1848 saw Kossuth as a key leader of the Hungarian revolution and he became head of the Committee of National Defence, finally being appointed provisional Governor of Hungary in 1849 – a position that was to be short-lived as internal dissension saw him resign and flee, initially to Turkey then on to London and No. 39 Chepstow Villas.

Notting Hill attracted residents from all over the world. Another person who settled in the area from abroad was William Henry Hudson, an Argentinian writer and naturalist of note. Born in 1841 he came to

England in 1869. Hudson wrote books on nature which included *Hampshire Days* and *Birds of London*. He changed discipline to write the romantic novel *Green Mansion* and the autobiographical *Far Away and Long Ago*. A bird sanctuary and sculpture of Rima (a character from his novel *Green Mansion*) was created to his memory in Hyde Park in 1925. His birthplace near Buenos Aires is a long way from his later home at 40 St Lukes Road.

Of course not all of the famous and infamous characters associated with the area actually lived here, which brings me to one that spent his last night alive in a basement flat in Lansdowne Crescent – Jimi Hendrix. Jimi Hendrix was born in 1942 in Seattle, Washington, US, and served in the American army as a paratrooper but was given an honourable discharge following an ankle injury. He moved to England in 1966 where he made his base. Hendrix burst onto the music scene with his revolutionary and unorthodox left-handed guitar playing. Hendrix did not use a left-handed guitar, but instead played a re-strung right-handed Fender Stratocaster. Tragically it was barely four years after arriving that he died from a drug overdose. James Marshall Hendrix died at Monika Dannerman's basement flat at 22 Lansdowne Crescent.

A well-known character of more recent times was the former wife of Band Aid organiser Sir Bob Geldof, Paula Yates. Paula was the daughter of broadcaster Jess Yates and had become famous as a presenter of cult TV show *The Tube* and later *The Big Breakfast*, in which she famously interviewed her guests in bed. Paula is fondly remembered by residents in the area following her tragic and untimely death from a heroin overdose in September 2000 at her St Lukes Mews home. The mews house was sold to a property investment firm in what must have been the quickest sale ever – it took three minutes from being listed on the estate agent's website. The purchaser paid £595,000 without even viewing the property or meeting the selling agent, 'They faxed us their bank details without even being shown around,' Winkworth's agent Alex Thompson is quoted as saying.

To talk about the famous that currently live in the area would require a separate book, not just a chapter. This is one of the facts that indicates the extent to which the neighbourhood is seen as the 'place to live in' and the 'place to be seen in'.

Commemorative plaque installed in 1991 to celebrate the 150th anniversary of the birth of W.H. Hudson.

Hudson's home very little change since this picture was taken in the late 1940s.

Argentinean writer and naturalist William Henry Hudson's home at No. 40 St Lukes Road, pictured in 2005.

The basement flat of Monika Dannerman at 22 Lansdowne Crescent, where rock legend Jimi Hendrix spent his last night.

Chapter 11
Small Screen, Big Screen, Music and the Written Word

The television, cinema, music and literary industries have found Notting Hill a splendid background for many a blockbuster, with one film in particular showcasing this part of North Kensington and making it the star – that film was of course the critically acclaimed *Notting Hill* staring Hugh Grant and Julia Roberts. However, read on, there is more... lots more.

When it comes to television, W11 has been represented on many occasions; it has been shown in dramas and reality projects. One person that has appeared in a documentary is Ninon Asuni, who was in a 2004 Channel Four production which showcased All Saints Road and its recent transformation from 'front line no go area' to its new community orientated image. Ninon owns and runs the bicycle shop in All Saints Road.

Over the years the news programmes have visited Notting Hill over and over again – in the 1950s it was Mosley and the racial tensions with its resulting riots. In the swinging 1960s it was the flower-power children that made the headlines. The 1970s saw protests over the Westway extension and the use of land under the elevated road, and near riots at the carnival which again brought unwanted media attention to Notting Hill. The 1980s were dominated with stories of drug and gang problems and, of course, the arrival of the biggest names in pop music joining together to raise money for the Ethiopian famine relief effort – it was of course Band Aid and 'Do They Know it's Christmas' recorded at the Island Studios in Basing Street. The record was heard and video shown over the Christmas of 1984, going straight to the number-one spot. It was re-released in 1985 and 1989, reaching number three and one respectively. The 1990s once again saw politicians fighting over the local votes, with heavyweights like Dennis Healey being seen on the streets of Notting Hill. After the turn of the millennium, 'the naughties' as they have become known, haven't lived up to their nickname – so far. Newswise things are, as they say in newspaper language, 'slow', with one notable exception – Band Aid. A new and updated version of the '80s record, which was again recorded in Basing Street, once more it went straight to number one, raising money for Africa's starving. Sir Bob Geldof and Midge Ure worked their magic again for a good cause.

On the big screen Notting Hill has really made a mark, with numerous films being either shot or based in London W11. In the 1960s Lionel Ngakane directed and produced the screenplay for the film *Jemima and Johnny*, a touching but frank film that was inspired by the Notting Hill race riots a decade earlier. It is a fine film in which Jemima and her parents arrive in Notting Hill as black immigrants. Johnny is white and the son of an active racist who distributes his racial literature around the area. The film is a story of the adventures of Jemima and Johnny, and how they end up in a derelict and dangerous house, 'Johnny's Den'. It is Johnny's father who rescues the youngsters and, for a brief moment, the racial tension is forgotten as both sets of adults realise the possible consequences of the children's play activities.

Made in black and white in 1966 the film was shot on location in Notting Hill. It is a film that was and is relevant in terms of its racial message. Ngakane has captured the tensions, problems and social commentary of the era and reflects the problems that he himself faced during the apartheid years in his native South Africa.

In the 1970 film *Performance*, Rolling Stone Mick Jagger plays the burnt-out rock star Turner opposite James Fox's gangster character Chas. The film is a masterpiece that was billed as a 'British Gangster' film, but it is much more than just that – it is crammed with hedonism, violence, drugs and rock 'n' roll. Finished in 1968 it took two years of cutting and negotiating before it was finally released. It was filmed in Notting Hill with its backdrop amongst the large houses of Colville Square, their white facades leaving one wondering if those sordid scenes are ever played out in real life. Both Jagger and Fox found the film disturbing – Fox didn't act for almost ten years after it and Jagger found himself in what he has described as an 'artistic slump'. It is a film that the producer Nicholas Roeg says he would rather forget.

There have been numerous films that have seen the streets of Notting Hill co-starring with international and British superstars, but the film that most people will remember is 'Notting Hill'. Hugh Grant, and Julia Roberts play characters that almost mirror their real life personas. The film is shot in and around Portobello Road, with the famous door scene being shot in Westbourne Park Road – although people still photograph the doorway the actual door was sold at auction to raise money for charity.

The second genre to be captivated by W11 is music, but it's not just mentioned in the lyrics – an entire industry has grown up in the borough. Many bands have made their debut in the area and two venues that crop up again and again are All Saints Church Hall in Powis Garden and the Free School in Powis Square.

The Basing Street studios, formerly the HQ and recording facility of Island Records.

The entrance to Vernon Yard, where Richard Branson founded the Virgin empire.

The venues saw super groups Pink Floyd and Quintessence, and solo artists like Tom Jones either practising or playing sets from the mid-1960s.

Having signed for Virgin the Sex Pistols drove around the area in a lorry, stopping to perform in the streets – it seemed to work as the group turned into what is probably the only punk 'super group'. Paul Cooke (drummer) and Steve Jones (guitar) went to Christopher Wren School over the border in Shepherd's Bush, W12.

There is one band that took things one step further by not only being seen in the area and record-ing locally but naming themselves after a road in the borough. They are All Saints who allegedly came up with the name whilst using the local café in All Saints Road during breaks in recording at a local studio.

As previously mentioned the Band Aid singles were both recorded in Basing Street with many stars performing on both recordings. Amongst the stars on the first single were Boy George, George Michael, Bananarama, Status Quo, Paul Young and Bono. The second recording in 2004 had Bono from the original recording singing the same lines and new stars like Katie Melua, Dizzy Rascal and The Darkness amongst the new ensemble. Also recording at the Island studios (now owned by Trevor Horne) over the years were Bob Marley, U2 and Free amongst others.

In terms of actual songs with a link to W11, they include Leo Sayer's 1974 song 'One Man Band', in which he proclaimed 'everybody knows down Ladbroke Grove you have to leap across the street, you can lose your life under a taxi cab...' Cat Stevens (later known as Yusef Islam) sang about Portobello Road on the 'B' side of 'I Love My Dog', while Van Morrison recalled the fact he lived in Ladbroke Grove on the track 'Slim Slow Slider', recorded with his Band 'Them'. Rock band Hawkwind were regular diners in the Mountain Grill Café at 275 Ladbroke Grove – they must have been served a good fry-up because their fifth LP was named after it, being called 'Hall of the Mountain Grill'.

The locality has been rich in recording studios as well as record labels and companies. Joe Meek, the legendary record producer, was a recording engineer in the 1950s at the Lansdowne studios which were located at 2 Lansdowne Road. Meek went on to produce some of the records that epitomise the late 1950s and early '60s including 'Telstar' by the Tornados, named after the newly-invented satellite that was making headlines in 1962.

Island Records was founded by Chris Blackwell in his native Jamaica in 1959 using just £100 and ended up being sold nearly 30 years later for undisclosed millions. Chris Blackwell came from a wealthy Jamaican family and is quoted as saying:

When I recorded Laurel Aitken and those people, I never thought it would be the start of a popular record company, I was just recording the music because I wanted to do it

and I loved it. Jamaica is a very small place and I was only thinking in simple terms at that stage.

The name Island is a reference to the Alec Waugh novel *Island in the Sun*, a favourite read of Chris Blackwell. Island Records did not have to wait long for success – it was soon riding high in the Jamaican charts with the Laurel Aitken song 'Boogie in my Bones', which was soon followed by the company's first album release 'Lance Heywood at the Half Moon'. The album's catalogue number was CB22, a reference to the fact that at the time Chris was still only 22 years of age.

Within just three years Chris Blackwell decided that he should move his record business out of Jamaica and into the UK – 'I chose to bring the busi-ness to England rather than the USA purely because of the huge Jamaican population here.' The move to London was financed with a $5000 loan and the promise of a town house rented from the Church of England commissioners, but one thing he wanted was to achieve an international platform for his music – London he believed would provide that.

It wasn't easy to start with, and legend has it that Chris Blackwell travelled around to record stores and blues parties hawking his wares from the back seat of an old Mini Cooper. He soon set up his studios in Basing Street in the old congregational chapel. The company went from strength to strength over the next few years and became legendary in the progres-sive rock forum. In the late 1960s the balance of 75 per cent Jamaican and 'R and B' material, and 25 per cent progressive rock was being reversed. The Island Records' list of artists reads like a who's who of pop music with such legends as the Spencer Davis Group, King Crimson, Bob Marley, Emerson Lake and Palmer, Free and many more passing through the hands of Chris Blackwell. The company was sold in

An early example of Blackwell's Island Record label.

Vernon Yard, the birthplace of Virgin Records.

The small artisan's house at the southern end of Portobello Road that was for a while occupied by George Orwell.

the late 1980s and has since moved to premises in neighbouring Hammersmith, but the music legacy remains in the studios that have seen such an incredible amount of talent over the years. At the time of writing another huge name in the music industry, Trevor Horne, is the latest incumbent of the old congregational chapel in Basing Street.

The area has also spawned a multi-national mega company – Virgin. But it's the musical part of the business we want to look at in this chapter. Richard Branson started his business empire in the late 1960s with the student magazine that had a weekly circulation of 50,000 copies, but it was the record business that Richard Branson set his sights on. In 1969 he planned a mail-order record shop and by the beginning of 1970 that had become a reality. His business was run from premises in Vernon Yard just off of the eastern end of Portobello Road. The business was so successful that he opened his first record shop in Oxford Street in 1971. The following year a record studio was opened in the Manor near Oxford and one year on again, the real empire was born – Virgin Records opened its own record label with the first signing being Mike Oldfield. His album 'Tubular Bells' was massive with tracks being used on films such as *The Exorcist*, as well as it being the biggest-selling album of the decade in its own right.

In 1977 Virgin took a risk on the biggest and most controversial punk band of the time. The Sex Pistols had already crashed on to the record scene but they needed a record deal and EMI and A&M wouldn't touch them, but Virgin appeared to be courting trouble and signed the band. With hindsight it was a shrewd move, as the Pistols became the biggest punk band around. It wasn't long before the Pistols and Branson would use controversy to their advantage by releasing the album 'Never Mind the B....cks', an album title that would see them in court. They won

their case and the record sold like hot cakes – yet another success for the Virgin empire.

Virgin where on a roll and continued to grow with new signings such as Phil Collins and Boy George and Culture Club. They also went international with a subsidiary in France before moving into all the major markets in the world, including the notoriously difficult US sector.

In books Notting Hill has turned up over and over again, the writers ranging from historians and novelists to people who simply love the history and ambience of the area. Some names we have never heard of and others that are internationally acclaimed literary celebrities. Authors of the calibre of G.K. Chesterton and George Orwell have had links with the area.

The historical work of reference *Notting Hill in Days Gone By*, written by Florence Gladstone, is a work that has been used by researchers and historians for the last 80 years. It is a work that documents the area from the wealth of Notting Hill to the poverty of Notting Dale up to the 1920s, and is an absolute gold mine of information. Fictional works of note include *The Napoleon of Notting Hill* by G.K. Chesterton, a book written in 1904, which could so easily have been lost had it not been for the insight of the publisher. Chesterton, who was planning his first novel, was down to his last ten shillings (or 50 pence today) when he went to visit a publisher in Fleet Street. Not wishing to look out of place he used the money to get a shave, have a substantial meal and demolish a bottle of wine before seeing the publisher. Being penniless but well fed and watered he gave an overview of the book which the publisher liked enough to agree a deal – a £20 advance that would be sent to Chesterton the following week. This arrangement did not suit Chesterton, who needed the money immediately. Incredibly, the publisher gave into the demands of the author and the rest, as they say, is history.

The story is set 80 years in the future, 1984, and the new king, Auberon Quinn, who is appointed by lottery, takes everything as a joke, including his own kingship. A main character is from Notting Hill and he rallies the local residents to form an army and join him in defending his neighbourhood.

As indicated the story is set in 1984 which is relevant of course to another writer with links to Notting Hill. George Orwell lived for a time at the top of Portobello Road but the irony is in his links with G.K. Chesterton, as it was he who gave Orwell his break. Some 20 years after writing *The Napoleon of Notting Hill* Chesterton published a work by Eric Blair in *G.K.'s Weekly*. Blair's pen name was George Orwell, who of course would go on to write the futuristic novel *1984* later in his career.

Even earlier than Chesterton, Charles Dickens made references to the area in his books with the Potteries and Hippodrome cropping up in *Bleak House*. Such was the reputation for poverty and unruly inhabitants at the time that when Dickens

wanted to include a piece of that nature he referred to Notting Dale in order to give an air of reality – it probably helped that this was an area that Dickens knew very well.

Charles Dickens junr also wrote about the area with Notting Hill and Dale being included in his book *Dickens's Dictionary of London 1888*, a work that documented life in Victorian London from the affluence of the west end to the slums and poverty of the Dale.

It would be impossible to précis or even list all the books that are relevant to, or set in Notting Hill, but I hope those mentioned here give a flavour and varied indication of what a rich genre this is.

I am consciously not including too many details of film locations and musical hot spots because the last thing I want is to turn this book into a rock, cinematic or literary gazetteer. Suffice to say that at almost every turn we can indicate a scene, song or chapter of note. Should this book whet your appetite for more information then please search out Tom Vague's psychogeography publications and the History Talk group – you will not be disappointed.

Above left: *Street entertainer outside the ground-floor bar on Talbot Road.*

Above: *Another guitarist entertains in Portobello Road near Lonsdale Road.*

Left: *The sound of the Caribbean near Westbourne Grove. This busker was working from his wheelchair.*

Looking across Kensington Gardens towards the round pond.

Right: A programme from the 1958 game against Fulham, the cost of which was four pennies (less than two new pence). On the Fulham side that day was football legend Johnny Haynes who was killed in a car crash during the writing of this book.

Below: Kensington Gardens, near the play area. The Elfin Oak is in the background.

Chapter 12

Not Quite Notting Hill, But Almost

I am aware that *The Book of Notting Hill* should be about Notting Hill, but I ask the reader to bear with me on this chapter. It seems to me that boundaries and areas are manmade, and in fact, as members of a community, we all travel outside and meet people from outside our own home base. It is simply this fact that has led me to write this chapter on some worthy items, people and organisations, just outside Notting Hill.

As a child I remember the summer holidays from school lasting an eternity – it was only six weeks, that's one and a half pay days in today's language, but we seemed able to cram so much in, which brings me to the first of the 'but almost' items.

A favourite play area for me, my sister Maureen and friends Cheryl and Angela Saunders was Kensington Gardens. My mother and her friend Jean Saunders would either walk or catch a double-decker bus to Bayswater Road. We would take our model yachts to the round pond, along with a packed lunch, and would sail the boats from one side to the other – sometimes they got caught up in the weeds that grew so prolifically in the pond. I think the 'parkies' got fed up with us kids harassing them to retrieve our treasured model yachts with the aid of a rowing boat. We would also go swimming in the lido located on the Serpentine.

The gardens are the setting for Kensington Palace, which was the birthplace of Queen Victoria who lived there from birth until she became queen in 1837. It was Queen Caroline, wife of King George II, who in 1728 moulded the gardens to the form they are today. She had the Serpentine and Long Water created from the Westbourne Stream (Bourne being an old English word for river or stream). The Serpentine (or the 'Serps', as it is known to locals) has become a leisure area for fishing, boating, swimming, relaxing and it is something to jog around, like one of its most famous visitors, Princess Diana used to do. Queen Victoria added the ornate Italian gardens and the Albert Memorial which stands opposite the Albert Hall.

Adjacent to the Serpentine is the statue of Peter Pan, the boy who never grew up. The statue is a bronze by Sir George Frampton and depicts Peter Pan playing pipes on top of a base covered in small animals. It was erected by J.M. Barrie, the author of *Peter Pan*, in 1912.

My favourite recollection of Kensington Gardens is seeing Spike Milligan (1918–2002) repainting the Elfin Oak in the mid-1960s. The Elfin Oak, which

was finally given a Grade II listing on 19 December 1997, is one of the most unusual items on the 'list of buildings of special architectural or historic interest', and is an absolutely charming piece of English curiosity and heritage. The weathered and gnarled oak stump came originally from Richmond Park and is thought to be some 800 years old. It was sculptured with elves, fairies and various animals over a two-year period by children's book illustrator Ivor Innes. The Elfin Oak is situated near the children's playground at Black Lion Gate, where it has stood since George Lansbury's interwar years' scheme for improvements to public amenities in 1930.

Notting Hill is well represented by sporting clubs, but for professional football we need to venture across the border into Shepherd's Bush for the first taste of a more physical side to our community. Queen's Park Rangers Football Club has a proud history which started not in Shepherd's Bush but over the northern border in Paddington. The club was founded in the St Judes Institute by the Droop Street Board School in 1882 and was known as St Judes. In 1886 the name Queen's Park Rangers was adopted because the club merged with Christchurch Rangers and most of the members came from the Queen's Park area. They played at various pitches and used four posts with tape for crossbars. By 1888 the had club moved to the London Scottish ground for a rent of £20 per annum, at which point they started charging admission. Using this ground for home fixtures was to be short-lived as the pitch became unplayable too easily. Between 1890 and 1892 the club moved around and used pitches in Kensal Green and Wormwood Scrubs, amongst others.

QPR's first silverware came in 1892 when they won the *West London Observer* Cup beating Fulham 3–2 – it was a cup they were to win again for the following two seasons.

In 1896, having won the London Cup the previous year, QPR moved grounds again, going to Kensal Rise Athletic Ground where an admission fee of 6d. ($2^1/_2$ pence) was charged. By 1898 the club needed to stop players leaving to join other clubs and so on 28 December the club turned professional and applied to join the Southern League. They played their first league match on 9 September at Tottenham, losing 1–0.

Again QPR spent the next few years moving from ground to ground, including a spell at Park Royal and White City, finally taking over Loftus Road from amateur club Shepherd's Bush just before the start of the 1920 season.

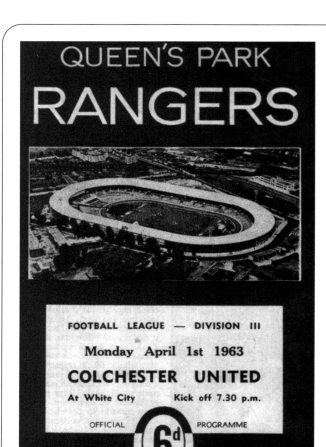

Above: *A ticket for the League Cup semi-final from February 1967.*

Left: *A QPR programme from 1963. The cover picture is of White City Stadium, the QPR home ground for a while.*

The West London Observer, *W11's local paper, was based in Latimer Road. Note the phone number with the area code 'PARK', which was short for Kensington Park, a throwback to the Kensington Park estate.*

League cup final programme for QPR vs West Bromwich Albion, at Wembley Stadium in March 1967.

It was 1921 before QPR were elected to the newly formed Third Division, and they finished third behind Crystal Palace and Southampton. The year 1926 saw the famous and much-loved blue and white hoops adopted as the club colours.

In 1952 the club installed floodlighting at Loftus Road at a cost of £5,000, with the first floodlit game being against Arsenal on 5 October. It wasn't until 1967 that QPR really hit the big time when the club battled their way to the final of the League Cup. It was the first time the League Cup final was to be played at Wembley and QPR would meet West Bromwich Albion, the cupholders from the First Division. At the time QPR were still playing in the Third Division. Notting Hill, as well as Shepherd's Bush, pulled out all the stops for the occasion and unusually the club coach toured the area on its way to Wembley for the game, receiving a rousing welcome. Mark Lazarus, who was a QPR hero of the time, is quoted as saying:

... even the coach journey was a wonderful experience, we toured the Willesden and Holland Park area and the fans lined the streets to wave and shout support.

The coach journey was just as amazing as actually winning. We just had to win, that was all there was to it. The support around Westbourne Park and Shepherd's Bush was unbelievable.

Fans walked to Wembley carrying a coffin to bury West Bromich Albion, and Notting Hill hero, World Boxing Champion and devoted QPR fan Terry Downs, painted his Rolls Royce car in blue and white stripes to celebrate the occasion.

West Bromich Albion went in at half-time with a 2–0 advantage with both goals being scored by ex-QPR player Clive Clarke. The second half was one of the greatest fight backs seen at Wembley. Roger Morgan scored the first, then the fans' favourite Rodney Marsh got the equaliser, and just before the final whistle Mark Lazarus made it 2–3 to QPR. They had become the first Third Division side to win a Wembley cup final, and in the same season won promotion to the Second Division. The Sunday after the cup final was surreal in Notting Hill and I remember getting up early to buy the Sunday papers to read about the match that I had been to the day before. I must confess to taking one of the newspaper posters from the billboard as a souvenir, a souvenir I still have along with the match programme which I have treasured for the last 39 years.

Since then the club has yo-yoed between the First and Second Divisions, with a short spell in the Premiership – one highlight was a cup final against Tottenham Hotspur in which QPR lost in a replay after drawing the first game.

A further connection between QPR and Notting Hill is one of the club's players. Les Ferdinand was brought up on the Lancaster West estate and honed his skills playing five-a-side football at the Harrow Club, where he played other local teams in the converted church which was the Harrow Mission. Les recalled in his autobiography 'sometimes the games got really serious', but being a youth in the area meant there was temptation on every street corner, playing football at the club 'meant we weren't hanging around the street and kept us away from the sort of problems you can get involved in when you

Les Ferdinand – QPR, England and Notting Hill hero.

get bored.' Les was a loyal player for his local club QPR and later went on to play for his country and premiership sides Newcastle United and Tottenham Hotspur. Les also played for Turkish club Besiktas, as well as West Ham United, Bolton Wanderers and Leicester City. Les was and has remained one of the area's great sporting heroes.

For many years my father, Alfred Wilkinson, worked just outside our area at the GPO's main sorting office adjacent to Paddington Station – what is remarkable about that I hear you say? Well nothing actually, but what I would like to mention is the fact that the GPO, or Royal Mail as it is now known, has it's very own underground railway at the sorting office. The railway threads its way from Paddington to the sorting office at Mount Pleasant in central London, which is no mean feat when you think what it has to avoid – sewers, drains, underground service conduits and even other underground train tunnels. The railway is an automated and unmanned system

and was used solely for transporting mail. Unfortunately, this private railway is no longer used. It was decommissioned in the late 1990s, putting more lorries on to the roads of London. What is ironic is that it was closed just as the London congestion charge was implemented.

It was always an adventure whenever I went with my father to Paddington, because no visit to that area was complete without a visit to the mainline station to see the fabulous steam trains of the Great Western Railway. Even from the concourse you could get that long-lost smell of the coal-fired locomotives. It was also a chance to catch up on the other form of transport that was in abundance in and around the station – the lorries and vans, British Railway's Scamell Scarabs, those funny three-wheeled articulated trucks and the fleets of bright red Royal Mail vans. We got there on the big red London double-decker buses. As a child it was quite an adventure and I have many memories of those days.

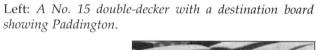
Left: *A No. 15 double-decker with a destination board showing Paddington.*

Right: *A Royal Mail van at Paddington. Note the cipher of King George on the vehicle's livery.*

Below: King Edward I *in steam at Paddington Station, December 2004.*

Chapter 13

The Biggest Carnival in Europe

If you listen to the Bob Marley record 'Trench Town Rock', the lyrics proclaim, 'one good thing about music, when it hits you, you feel no pain.' Well, take it from me I have stood in front of some of the sound systems that are used at the Notting Hill carnival and I can tell you the bass levels are such that they can take your breath away. You can feel the beat hammering your chest and your ears ring for a long time after you move away – at carnival you really can feel the music. The atmosphere is absolutely electric, the smells of the foods are heavenly and the dancers are beautiful. Carnival takes over parts of Notting Hill during the bank holiday weekend in August with the biggest day being bank holiday Monday.

Notting Hill Carnival? Well, yes it is now, and it came about probably as a direct result of the Notting Hill race riots. It was an attempt to heal wounds between the black and white communities, but the first carnival took place in the more central location of St Pancras Town Hall in 1959. The event was held indoors as a direct result of the weather – carnival in Trinidad is traditionally held in February and so it was in England. February in London is about a far away from sunny days of the Caribbean as you can get. The festivities were the brainchild and were organised by Claudia Jones, who had been part of the black civil rights movement in the US and editor of the *West Indian Gazette*. For the next few years the carnival was held in a number of different locations until 1964, when thanks to Rhuane Laslett, a local social worker, carnival came to Notting Hill. You have to wonder if these two visionaries could possibly have guessed what an international success those early gatherings would become.

To understand why the carnival is so huge and means so much to Notting Hill, especially the Afro-Caribbean community, you need to know its history, traditions and indeed its rules. Carnival has a history of over 200 years in Trinidad, being transported to Spanish-held Trinidad by French colonials in the 1780s. The tradition was upheld under British rule by the white landed classes as a European-style festival with the free coloureds and slaves taking no part. It was adopted by the black masses of Trinidad as an expression of their new-found freedom following the Abolition of Slavery Act in 1833. It is worth remembering that, at that time, Notting Hill and Notting Dale were no more than a couple of farms and rolling fields. From the 1830s Trinidad became the spiritual home of carnival but it soon spread, firstly throughout the Caribbean and then across the globe. Carnival is a

tradition that is upheld wherever you find communities of Afro-Caribbean people. The native communities have gained from the culture and the happiness it brings – it is a coming together of races, creeds, colours and religions.

When you attend the carnival there is a feeling that chaos may break out at any moment, but the organisation of an event on this scale is such that invariably the whole event goes off without a hitch, or so it seems to those enjoying the spectacle. It is also easy to think that there are no rules, but there are. There are five disciplines that were established in, and have travelled from, the home of carnival, Trinidad. The five disciplines are:

1. *MAS. This is the costume or masquerade processions with lavish floats that make such good TV.*
2. *CALYPSO. This is the traditional Trinidadian music.*
3. *SOCA. An upbeat and energetic form of Calypso*
4. *STEELPAN. These are the traditional instruments of Trinidad and are made from oil drums.*

A young carnival-goer on her father's shoulders enjoys the spectacle outside the Earl of Lonsdale, at the junction of Portobello Road and Westbourne Grove.

(COURTESY OF DUNCAN GRISBY)

Above: *Young participants of the MAS parade, 2005.*

Left: *The carnival in 2003. Crowds watch as the participants pass wearing their huge head-dresses.*
(COURTESY OF DUNCAN GRISBY)

Ladbroke Grove at the junction with Lancaster Road, looking towards the Hammersmith and City Line bridge in 2003.
(COURTESY OF DUNCAN GRISBY)

A young participant of the children's carnival gets some well-deserved attention from the press – the police officer also seems to be enjoying it. (COURTESY OF DUNCAN GRISBY)

'It's been a long day, but I've really enjoyed the carnival.' It's what carnival is all about. (COURTESY OF LADY ORANGE)

5. *STATIC SOUND SYSTEMS. More of a Jamaican invention, the sound systems play various types of music with the emphasis on Reggae. However, more modern forms such as hip hop, rap etc. are now enjoyed by the revellers.*

One great success at the carnival is the children's section which sees the youngest members of the community doing all the things the adults do. They come from schools, clubs and other organisations and create costumes for the Mas parade that are equally as intricate and colourful (and sometimes nearly as enormous) as the adult versions. And there are junior steel bands and dancers, as well as those who are just out to enjoy the atmosphere.

One of the traditions, if not rules, of carnival is that everyone, be they pensioners or small children, must enjoy themselves. It is also one of the rules that is wholeheartedly embraced by anyone and everyone attending the August bank holiday event. I can honestly say that almost 100 per cent of photographs seen in papers and on TV contain happy faces, and on only a few occasions can I remember any degree of trouble. The safety record and success in controlling an event of this size owes everything to the dedication and professionalism of the carnival committee and its helpers, along with sympathetic policing. The Notting Hill Carnival has become a celebration of London's multicultural and multinational make up and is a success story that has been copied, but as yet it hasn't been bettered.

When I have spoken to people about the carnival it's a shame that to hear about the troubles of 1976. It seems that everybody remembers those few incidents but while talking to Victor Fergus, a man that has been in England and indeed Notting Hill since 1960,

I got a different perspective. I asked Victor if he thought the troubles had bonded the community together:

I think that people read that carnival trouble completely wrong – don't misunderstand me it was bad, it was very bad, but if you take a step back and take a look you see that the same sort of thing happened in Birmingham, Manchester and Bristol etc. so it wasn't just a community thing, it was something in society that was bubbling under for a long time and it had to come out. Unfortunately for us it came out at carnival. So to answer your original question, now that the issues that caused the problems in various communities have been addressed, as a result of the trouble, yes it has bonded our community.

Ray Berkem lived in All Saints Road during the late 1970s and '80s and was involved with the local workers' socialist party and housing co-ops, but his mind goes back to the time he was selling books from of the Socialist Workers' stall located under the Westway on Portobello Road:

It was carnival and a colleague and I were doing our bit for the SWP by selling books just off the Lane under the flyover. Thinking back there had been a bit of an atmosphere all day, nothing specific had happened apart from a couple of kids had been arrested for nicking handbags or something, but by late afternoon we knew something was going to happen. Not long before we were going to pack up we heard shouting and a commotion and all of a sudden all the black kids seemed to be running at us. They were hitting and kicking anyone or anything in their way we had no choice – we had to do a runner ourselves but my colleague tripped up. I thought he was going to be trampled so I grabbed him by the collar and picked him up. All he was worried about was the books, but believe me for a moment I thought I had had it. The book stall went flying but we managed to get out

Time for a refreshment break.

of the way, fortunately. I think it was probably the start of the trouble because by the early evening gangs were roaming around causing trouble and fighting the police all over the area. In the cold light of day a lot of people thought it could have been the end of carnival, or at least turning it into some sort of arena event, but the authorities and organisers got together and got it back on track.

That was in 1976 and fortunately it was the only real trouble to stain the reputation of the Notting Hill Carnival. Everyone involved with the event works hard to ensure that the scenes we saw then do not

reoccur and the one and a half million visitors have an enjoyable and safe carnival.

In 1981 the carnival was again to make the headlines of the national papers, when a plot to sabotage both the event and the good relations between black, white communities and the police in the area, and probably the whole country, was being hatched by extremists. Neo Nazis had planned a two-pronged assault on the event with a bomb and sniper attack. It is very fortunate that that particular event was foiled before anybody was hurt and the good nature of the carnival maintained.

So who comes to carnival? Well according to people I have spoken to, just about anyone. Bess Gordon is another person that came to England from the Caribbean. She arrived in Notting Hill in 1957 as a young lady from Jamaica, so she is someone that has seen the carnival grow into what it is today. Bess told me about the revellers that come to carnival:

I meet all kinds of people at carnival, people that live in the area, people that come from all over England and people from further away, but its amazing – I have seen many of those people year after year, they talk to us one year then the next say hello because they remember us. Sometimes they ask to rest outside our home or to use the toilet – that's nice and of course we don't mind helping them out.

The volume of revellers at the carnival in 2003 is illustrated by this picture of the crowds in Ladbroke Grove. The spire of St John the Evangelist can be seen in the distance.
(Courtesy of Duncan Grisby)

Chapter 14

Black Culture and the Arrival
of the Caribbean Immigrants

The arrival of the first Caribbean immigrants into Notting Hill was a landmark in the area's history, but where, apart from the Caribbean, did it all start and more importantly where has it taken the community?

A name that is almost synonymous with the early arrival of the black immigrants into this country is the troop ship the *Empire Windrush*. It is a name that springs readily to mind, but the ship is one thing and the people another.

The new arrivals came to these shores in their lightweight suits and wide-brimmed hats – even though the welcome was warm to start with the climate certainly wasn't. The neighbourhoods they went to in London, Birmingham, Nottingham and other areas must have seemed a world away from their own sun-drenched islands. They were greeted with rain, fog and cold winds. These people had been brought to this country at the invitation of the British government, as British subjects, to help run the understaffed railways, hospitals, buses and other public services. Many of the new arrivals found themselves working on the building sites of post-war cities that had been devastated by German bombing, but finding work was one thing and finding accommodation was something else. Why were these new immigrants different? Well, for one thing, they stood out from the crowd. I can remember seeing the first members of the Afro-Caribbean communities around the streets of Notting Hill, streets that were strewn with rubbish and lined with dilapidated houses. The local white community were already having a hard time; rationing hadn't long finished, housing was overpriced and in poor condition. Please don't get me wrong, I am not trying to make excuses for the way

these new arrivals were treated, but with the set of circumstances that prevailed at that time it was probably inevitable that the social situation could become tense. Indeed, the influx of a different type of people has always been a problem, from the times of the gypsies, Irish railway workers and Jews etc. I think this group found it difficult to understand why they were treated the way they were. We must remember that the war was not long over and many of the new arrivals had been welcomed to the British armed forces – 10,000 West Indians volunteered when the Second World War broke out. At the time there were very few black people in England. There was even a squadron in the RAF called the Jamaica Squadron, named after the island that had paid for the planes. After the war most of the West Indian servicemen went back to the Caribbean, but some decided to stay on in the Forces. In 1947, 250 of these men went home on leave, and they had to wait six months before a ship could be found to return them to their units. The ship that was diverted to the Caribbean was the SS *Empire Windrush*, which had a capacity to carry 1,000 passengers and set sail for England on 24 May 1948.

When the ship docked at Tilbury on 22 June the passenger list was made up of some 250 servicemen returning to duty, with the remaining spaces being occupied by young men that had snapped up one-way tickets from the ship's operators. These young men had journeyed to England looking for adventure and employment, and the fare was £28.10s. However, they were in for a challenging time in their new home. They were people who had been brought up in the Caribbean as British subjects – their schools

The troop ship SS Empire Windrush, *probably the most important vessel in the history of the Caribbean immigrants.*

Adverts for passage to the UK taken from Jamaican newspapers.

121

Caribbean servicemen who volunteered during the Second World War.

were modelled on British schools, the union flag was their flag and they respected the royal family with a passion. Not many of these migrants knew anyone in this country or had anywhere to stay. The authorities decided to house them temporarily in the underground shelters of Clapham Common, for which they were charged two shillings a night, with the condition that they left as soon as they found employment. The first stop in the quest for work was the labour exchange, with the nearest being in Brixton, just up the road. The migrants did not take long to find work, as in post-war England the lack of able-bodied men to replace the wartime female workers meant jobs outnumbered workers – the new arrivals simply went to where the jobs were – Manchester, the Midlands and London. There were stories of black workers leaving a job at lunchtime and being re-employed somewhere else before the end of the day.

The *Windrush* migrants settled in and established themselves in the UK. The government of the day realised that this was a ready-made labour pool for the understaffed railways, buses and hospitals, and it didn't take long for the authorities to run recruiting drives, even sending staff to the Caribbean to encourage migrants to England. The success of this initiative was such that during the 1950s over a quarter of a million West Indians came to England.

The expectations of these people was far from reality – the weather was cold, but it was the welcome from the people that really made these people feel homesick. They found that, unlike in the West Indies, where people greeted one and other with a cheerful good morning or hello, in England speaking to someone would usually get no response except a puzzled look. As the number of migrants increased then so did the level of animosity, and by the early 1950s there were significant West Indian communities in most major cities. In London it was Brixton and of course Notting Hill, but these people began to feel more and more isolated. The immigrants tended to be young single males who naturally sought female company – this added a new dimension when

The shop in Blenheim Crescent which in 1958 was Totobags West Indian Café and Blues Club. It was here that the Notting Hill race riots really came to a head.

the young white males saw them with white girls. It was no fun for the girls either – very often they were shunned by their own families and communities.

Housing was another problem. Peter Rachman was making a fortune from the black immigrants, charging between a guinea and £1.10s. for a space in a room, which meant that you shared a single room with two or three other people, usually complete strangers. Although the conditions were appalling those that took his rooms were still grateful to Rachman, as he was the only person that would supply accommodation. That said, however, many got on the wrong side of Rachman and his henchmen. His methods were such that if you didn't pay your rent you could find your belongings on the street and someone else in your bed on your return from work. There was always someone looking for accommodation.

With the increase in racial tension, intolerance and consequently the increase in the level of violence, it was inevitable that these circumstances would culminate in the worst race riots seen in England – it was 1958 and Notting Hill was set to explode. Notting Hill was not the scene of the first race riots of 1958 – the two weeks or so preceding the Notting Hill riots saw tensions erupt into violence on the streets of Nottingham. Some believed it was inevitable that this would spread elsewhere, and the first seeds of violence were sown on 23 August, the same night that Nottingham was struggling with racial violence. In Notting Hill nine white youths had gone looking for black victims. They drove around and over a period of some four hours were involved in about five incidents. The next few days saw tensions rise and the following weekend, a hot bank holiday weekend, was to witness some of the worst incidents that North Kensington has ever seen.

The trouble started on the Friday night when a crowd gathered near Latimer Road Station in Notting Dale. The catalyst was an argument between a black man named Raymond and his white girlfriend, Majbritt, a Swedish girl – that was all that was needed for trouble to start. The following night the crowd gathered and confronted Majbritt again – it appeared that the crowd wanted blood. The police were slow in arriving but when they did they took Majbritt into protective custody, but not until she had been attacked and hit with an iron bar. With their intended victim taken out of harm's way the crowd, still wanting blood, went on the rampage, attacking any black people they came across.

Over the next two nights the streets of Notting Hill saw mobs in an absolute frenzy of racial hate. This had never been seen in England before and sent shock waves through the community and authorities. The black community was withdrawing into its homes. A young West Indian named Seymour Manning, who had come down to London to visit friends, wandered straight into the middle of this volatile situation. He was immediately targeted by a gang of Teddy boys who chased him until he gained shelter in a greengrocers shop. Manning avoided serious injury, but it was clear something was going to happen and it was felt that the black community must defend themselves.

Preparations were made on bank holiday Monday at a blues club in Blenheim Crescent. Molotov cocktails and various weapons were stockpiled and the young black men waited for the mobs to find them. Their wait wasn't in vain and, sure enough, in the early evening a crowd gathered in between Portobello Road and Kensington Park Road, but those inside Totobags West Indian Café were ready. Amongst those West Indians was Michael de Freitas, Baron Baker and Frank Crichlow, and they were intent on defending their community, so as the tension grew and the crowd got agitated they tossed their fire bombs at the crowd. With reinforcements from other parts of London the police battled to regain control. A black Mariah police van was used to block the doors of the club at No. 9 Blenheim Crescent, to stop those inside coming out to fight, but not until after Baker, de Freitas, Crichlow and six other black males were arrested and three whites are taken into custody – all were charged with affray. What was clear was that it wasn't just gangs of white youths that were intent on trouble, but the whole of the W11 community. If not active, they were probably complicit by their lack of verbal or active opposition to what was happening.

The gang of nine white youths whose violent attacks on blacks had signalled the start of these riots were convicted of a number of violent offences and

sentenced to four years in prison – sentences that were given as an indication that racial violence would not be tolerated. The repercussions of the riots would be felt for the next two decades, with relations between the black community and the police suffering, as did interracial relations within Notting Hill. It is into this climate that, as a measured and poignant gesture of support for the West Indian community, the Jamaican Chief Minister Norman Manley flew to England from the Caribbean. At the same time the English government did little but blame others, including the Jamaican government, for the problems and asked that they curb emigration.

The riots had brought a lot of the problems facing the entire community in Notting Hill to the nation's attention, but at the top of the list was housing. For years landlords, including Rachman, had exploited the most vulnerable in the community, and an awful lot of them were the Afro-Caribbean immigrants. These people, unlike the other communities, had an answer – they set up a type of money union where all members would pay in and then borrow against their payments to get deposits for their own housing. It was a system that worked and got a lot of those people out of the property trap.

One thing that came about as a direct result of the race riots of 1958 was the Notting Hill Carnival. It may have taken a number of years but the connection is clear. However, it is not the carnival, but those with foresight and courage, who are acknowledged in this chapter.

It is well documented that Claudia Jones was the mother of the Notting Hill Carnival, but who was Claudia Jones? Claudia was a feminist, political activist, community leader, Black Nationalist, communist and journalist – all of which she pursued with commitment and vigour. She conducted her struggle for equal rights during the difficult part of the twentieth century, but adversity in the face of this struggle just made her stronger.

Claudia was born in Trinidad in 1915 but moved with her family to the United States, setting up home in New York where she lived for 30 years. Claudia was plagued by ill health for most of her life. TB damaged her lungs and serious heart disease made life difficult, but she would not give in to such things or allow them to interrupt her calling or enthusiasm. During her years in New York she was a member of the American Communist Party, which allowed her to use her journalistic and community leadership skills to their full potential. At the age of 33 she was editor of 'Negro Affairs' for the communist party's publication the *Daily Worker,* and was well respected and listened to as a speaker, concentrating on human and civil rights. Her stay in the US ended in 1955 when she was deported by the American authorities – she was given asylum in England and immediately went about working with the Afro-Caribbean community

Black American activist and visitor to Notting Hill, Malcolm X.

in her newly adopted home of London. Claudia founded and edited the *West Indian Gazette*, a publication that was at the forefront of her fight for equal rights for the black community. It was a paper that she personally steered through financial problems and prejudice.

Claudia Jones lost her fight with poor health in 1964 but her lasting legacy is, and always will be, the carnival which she helped to launch in 1959. The slogan of the carnival is 'A peoples art is the genesis of their freedom.' The success of the event as a showcase for the artistic talents of the community encapsulates this philosophy.

The arrival of the Afro-Caribbean people on these shores was not only heralded by the violence in Notting Hill and Nottingham but also by the sunny sound of their music. The first taste of the music was given by a young man from Trinidad who was interviewed immediately on disembarking from the SS *Empire Windrush* at Tilbury. The young man was a calypso singer who went by the name of Aldwyn Roberts (aka 'Lord Kitchener') and he broke into song whilst being interviewed for *Pathé News*. Lord Kitchener gave a rendition of one of his own compositions entitled 'London is the Place For Me'. However, this was not the last time he was heard singing calypso. Lord Kitchener went on to record for Chris Blackwell's burgeoning Island Records label with his best-known contribution being a tune called 'Dr Kitch'.

The Caribbean community was made up of happy and vibrant people who enjoyed relaxing in the same way they had in their home countries. To this end 'shabeens' grew up in various parts of the borough. A shabeen is an illegal drinking club, usually held in a private dwelling, and of course the music of choice was blue beat, ska or calypso, washed down with cans of 'long-life' beer.

Music is a theme that has run through the Caribbean story from the start and it is not losing any of its impact, even today. It has gone from the calypsos of Trinidad through blue beat and ska to reggae

and now rap, with the strains of these sunny genres being heard loud and clear on the streets of Notting Hill. The carnival perpetuates these artforms with the sound systems blasting the infectious reggae beat or the hard-hitting raps from the youth of the area. The floats carry the steel bands and soca groups while the fabulously decked-out costume dancers buzz around the parade going from street to street on the carnival route.

The roots of black culture run deep in Notting Hill – many of those involved in racial equality found their way to the streets of the area they may have only been visiting, but their presence simply boosted the confidence of the Afro-Caribbean community. Amongst those that came and settled in the neighbourhood one in particular had a name that is synonymous with the racial equality movement of both America and later the UK. Amy Ashwood Garvey was the first wife of Marcus Garvey. She married him at the age of 17 – even at that tender age she was already a powerful public speaker, social worker and was clearly a woman who was destined to be a key figure in the world of racial matters. She was the first member of the UNIA (Universal Negro Improvement Association) which had been founded in 1914 by her future husband, Marcus. Amy later joined Garvey in the US where, in 1919, they were married at the Liberty Hall in Harlem. She became associate editor of the *Negro World* and was an officer of the Black Star Line and the Negro Factories Corporation. Although she and Garvey divorced she remained a particularly active member of the Pan-African movement. Marcus Garvey was later deported from the US after investigations by J. Edgar Hoover in 1927. By 1935 he had settled in Fulham where died in 1940. Amy Ashwood Garvey also found her way to England and took up residence in Notting Hill where she found herself in the midst of a racial struggle once more. Following the race riots of 1958 she set up the Association for the Advancement of Coloured People from her home. The house in Bassett Road, which is just off Ladbroke Grove, became an important meeting place for black women in the area, amongst whom was Claudia Jones.

Not all the prominent black figures that came to Notting Hill lived locally, and indeed some only made fleeting visits. Muhammad Ali (formerly Casius Clay) toured the area visiting the Free School in Powis Square at the invitation of Michael de Freitas. Around the same period de Freitas also brought Malcolm X and Sammy Davis junr to visit the area, visiting the Powis Square project that he was deeply involved in.

As for my own memories of prominent black cultural figures, it was back in around 1961 that Paul Robeson was invited to Colville School to present awards at the school prizegiving. The school choir sang one of Robeson's best-loved songs before the ceremony – the words and music of 'Mama's Little Baby

Loves Shortening Bread' rang out in the school hall. Of course the six-year-old voices could not match the deep baritone splendour of Paul Robeson's own rendition. I wish I could remember more about the occasion, but what I can remember is collecting my prize of a book from Paul Robeson. It was quite an occasion.

Of all the forms of art the one that typifies the black community of Notting Hill is music. It is a beat that has run through the community ever since the immigrants arrived on these shores. From the first sounds of calypso and blue beat to the ragga and rap of today, we have heard it on the streets during carnival, from the sound systems at weddings and parties and from virtually all the open windows of W11 on any sunny day. I, as a child, was so envious of my coloured friends because, unlike the white kids' parents, their parents loved and played the same music as them. Today's musical heroes, such as Bob Marley and the Wailers, and Aswad, have recorded their music in and around the area. The Island studios in Basing Street have been a magnet for both new talent and established superstars over the years. Blackwell, who set up the record label, had made his mark in Jamaica prior to coming to Notting Hill by recording such reggae legends as Laurel Aitken.

Of course one part of black culture that we have not fully examined is the culture of sport. At least two of this country's favourite sports personalities come from Notting Hill – the first was Daley Thompson who competed in a number of Olympic Games and won gold in two of them. He won gold in probably the hardest event in the games, the decathlon, an event that is considered to be the supreme challenge of physical achievement. Daley was born in Notting Hill and attended Colville School, and was one of the areas most respected and best-loved sons.

The second sporting icon, who also represented his country and played for a number of top clubs, was football legend 'Sir Les' Ferdinand. Les was raised on the Lancaster West estate and played his early football at the Harrow Club in Freston Road and for non-league club Hayes. He was a painter and decorator before he started his football career in 1987 with local club Queen's Park Rangers, over the border in Shepherd's Bush. He went on to play for his country 17 times and represented other clubs such as Tottenham Hotspur, West Ham United and Newcastle United. His career also took him away from England to play for Turkish club Besiktas. He was a great ambassador for his clubs, country and the community he came from. 'Sir Les', as he is known by the football fans that idolise him, has at last received an honour – Les received an MBE from Prince Charles in 2005. Les commented, 'receiving this

A 1970s flyer advertising the Q Club in Paddington.

award at the palace is like running out on to the pitch at Wembley, except that here you know no one is going to be booing.' Les gave up his playing career in 2004, having suffered many injuries and going through 14 different medical procedures. At the time of writing he is working with Watford FC on a non-contractual basis as part-time coach, but Les may even put his boots on again if needed at some point.

So where is black culture at now? Well, carnival is the biggest showcase of black culture and art in Europe, the costumes are the most visible statement of the Caribbean culture and the music of the steel bands and sound systems are the most audible. However, the local schools, community centres, colleges and art centres also cater for and create art and artists of every genre. There is poetry and painting everywhere, there are films and sculptures – in fact every branch of the arts is represented and enhanced by the Caribbean influence that emanates from almost every street in Notting Hill.

It isn't only the ordinary people that acknowledge the contribution that the Afro-Caribbean community has made to the area, and indeed the country, but also HRH The Prince of Wales. I quote from a speech given at the SS *Windrush* 50th anniversary reception at St James's Palace in June 1998:

I attach huge importance to the distinctive contribution which you, your families and the wider black community make to British life. In both the Houses of Parliament; in business; in local government; in the arts and literature; entertainment and the media; and in sport. And in thousands of less glamorous but – if I may say so – quite as worthwhile ways; in what we rather glibly call 'ordinary jobs' and bringing up 'ordinary' families.

These pictures are from Tony Sleep's series of images, 1974–82. The area of Freston Road was first squatted in the early 1970s and declared independent in 1977, becoming the 'Free and Independent Republic of Frestonia'.

Peace and tranquillity in the heart of Frestonia.

A landscape of partially demolished streets and high-rise housing, but to Frestonians tidying up was still important.

Chapter 15
Local Folklore, Demonstrations
or Just Interesting

Whenever you speak to people in London W11 they always have interesting, amusing or just plain daft stories about the area. I thought it would be worthwhile to compile these stories, as many have become almost folklore. Whenever people gather they seem to be able to almost magically delve into their memories and come up with these little gems.

On one such occasion the shy and retiring Rod Freeman and outgoing and flamboyant Tony Allen remembered the setting up of an independent state within North Kensington. Rod and Tony seemed to be able to talk to each other without actually speaking – the conversation only touched on the story which left me wanting more, and the only way to find out more was to do a little bit of my own research into Frestonia, as it was known. I think the two of them enjoyed whetting my appetite and then leaving me wondering if it was a wind up. Well I'm glad to report it was for real and here's the story.

The story of the 'Free and Independent Republic of Frestonia' started in the early 1970s, although at the time no one involved could have believed they would be embarking on such an exciting and even successful journey of social learning. The areas along the new A40(M) Westway extension consisted of vacant land that was earmarked for industrial redevelopment and houses which had been emptied and were awaiting demolition. However, industry was not queuing up to move in and the local authorities were in no hurry to clear the remaining houses on the site. This part of Notting Dale (Latimer Road) had always been particularly poor. It is the area that had been known as the Piggeries and was home to the armies of navvies and totters in earlier times. The totters had their stables and yards in the land now under and adjacent to the Westway, and all had been demolished in the compulsory purchase scheme implemented for clearing the way for the construction of the A40(M). The southern end of Latimer Road, now renamed Freston Road, was somewhat inevitably becoming inhabited by squatters. Squatting in North Kensington was becoming particularly fashionable and the sheer number of decaying and empty properties led to an ample supply of houses for the many needy and homeless people coming into the area.

The squatters consisted of musicians, artists, students, single parents and families – just about anyone who was in need of a roof over their head – in fact all the types of people that go to make up a community, and that is exactly what was being built

up. The houses had communal gardens, a crèche and even an art gallery, but the Greater London Council (GLC) had no intention of leaving this fledgling community to flourish and grow. In 1977, a boom time for British industry, the GLC announced that it had decided to lease off the entire area for industrial development and that all the remaining residential buildings were to be demolished. Public meetings were hastily called amongst the local residents and, not surprisingly, votes were cast and the people agreed to oppose the new plans for the area. This new and curious alliance of local residents and squatters decided on an unusual course of action to bring their plight to the attention of the media, and hence the public at large. In a plan that was reminiscent of the British comedy film 'Passport to Pimlico', the Frestonia residents committee announced to the UN, EEC, GLC and the British government that 'due to their long history of mismanagement of Frestonia, they had forfeited their right to determine the future of the area.' A protest of such a form as declaring independence was bound to attract attention from the world media, and attention was found in abundance as film and news crews descended on the area. Media attention is the oxygen a protest of this type needs to be successful, and success was to be the outcome of their fight. What had been developed in Frestonia was a community, and a community that would not lay down and die. In due course the squatters were given an amnesty and the dwellings earmarked for demolition given a reprieve. The local community set up the Bramley Housing Co-operative to work closely with the Notting Hill Housing Trust in designing and managing a new housing development.

From the fabulous set of photos by local photographer and former Frestonian minister Tony Sleep. Whatever the circumstances, some Frestonians made an effort to make their homes inhabitable.

Totters were a common sight on the streets of Notting Dale. Tom stabled his horse in the communal garden of Frestonia and made efforts to sell his wares on St Anns Road.

A modern interpretation of Frestonia with new office accommodation and trees.

A landmark of Frestonia. However, the décor, as well as the internal layout, was changed on a regular basis.

Avondale Park, site of the body of putrid stagnant water known as the 'Ocean'.

In 1985 the development was completed and the first of the Frestonians moved in. It was, and still is, an example of co-operation between residents, housing trusts and local authorities that is a pleasant and peaceful oasis of thoughtfully and sympathetically designed dwellings amongst the high-rise concrete structures of modern-day housing developments. It appears that, if not Frestonia itself, the spirit of Frestonia lives on in this special and historic part of Notting Dale.

At this point I thought I had finished with Frestonia but a search for photographs opened up a whole new treasure-chest of information and interesting facts. I found a website belonging to London photographer and former Frestonian Tony Sleep. I was simply looking for pictures of dilapidated houses and rubbish-strewn streets, but what I found were the faces and the personal lives of Frestonia. Tony Sleep had taken many pictures during the eight years he lived in squats in Freston Road and doubts that he would ever have become a professional photographer if it were not for 'the freedom from rent and the cupboard darkroom no landlord would have allowed.' He did, however, take away an experience that has clearly left a mark on his life. He has experience of communal living and of community and he, like so few, can also say he was briefly a minister of state for Frestonia.

Amongst the 120 citizens of Frestonia was actor David Rappaport who became the Foreign Minister. David would routinely take advantage of the media frenzy and charged £50 a time for interviews – clearly he was honing his entrepreneurial skills before unleashing himself on an unsuspecting entertainment industry.

On declaring independence all the citizens took the name Bramley, as did David who became David Rappaport-Bramley. This is not as daft as it may at first seem as this meant, should they at any point be evicted, the council would be compelled to re-house them as one big family.

David Rappaport died in 1990 and is sadly missed for his talent and ability to make people laugh.

During the early stages of declaring independ-ence the 'Free and Independent Republic of Frestonia' asked that a United Nations peace-keeping force be sent to Frestonia in anticipation of the authorities attempting to repossess the ramshackle group of dwellings.

By 1982 Tony Sleep had had enough – by then he had a son and realised that perhaps other Frestonians had also begun to give up on the ideals they had fought for. Outsiders had started to use the area for the wrong reasons – drug dealing, theft and violent crime were becoming the norm. This was an atmosphere a young family could do without. Some of the Frestonians did stay on and moved into the new developments. In recent years the drug dealers have mostly gone and the derelict houses have been cleared. What remains is a new development, a communal garden and, thankfully, a place in history. The musicians, artists, artisans, musical-instrument makers, single, married, young and old all played their part in this story and now I know these citizens and what they looked like – to me they have become people, not just an invisible entity.

Nicholas Albery was also a founder resident and minister in the Frestonian assembly. He was one of those who argued for and represented the people of the independent state. He was the son of Sir Donald Albery, impresario and theatre owner who had dropped out of college. He had travelled to San Francisco where he joined with the psychedelic movements that were still a feature of the era.

He was a prolific writer of poetry and a particularly active social inventor, and an activist with a passion for walking. Ironically he had never owned a car but died in a car crash at the age of 52 in 2001.

The name of Frestonia lives on. Look it up on the internet – there are other communities with the name and, who knows, maybe even the same ideals. There is music and in the home of Frestonia, Latimer Road, there is a business complex named Frestonia. The pictures of Frestonia and its citizens have been donated by Tony Sleep.

For those of us old enough to remember Oswald Mosley, we will usually associate him with the racial tension of Notting Hill in the late 1950s, but not all of the activities he organised or was involved in were of this nature. Tony Rawlings was born in 1947 in Kensington Park Road where he lived for many years. He recalls:

... just up the road, probably no more than 200 yards on the other side Mosley had his office. I can still see him now, he always waved when he see us kids. It was about 1957 or '58 and we would go out on the Mosley van to various meetings. It was an old Austin pick up. On one particular day Malcolm Morrison and me went on a march to Kensington town hall. It was an all-out union movement march with the Mosley men carrying union movement flags and banging drums, but the thing was they were also carrying two or three dustbins full of rubbish. The protest was to complain about the council cancelling one of the two weekly rubbish collections. They had a slogan for the march 'rubbish for rubbish' but when we got to the town hall the Mosley men stormed in and threw the rubbish all over the reception area. I don't think it done a lot of good but we thought we were putting the world to rights as young kids.

The town hall was the scene of many demonstrations and delegations from the late 1950s through to the early '70s, with causes ranging from rubbish collections, poor housing, poverty and even the lack of laundry facilities.

It was in 1973 when the local ladies got heated over the issue of laundry facilities in the Lancaster and Silchester Road area. Notting Dale Laundry Campaign, as it became known, was the result of the Westway extension and slum clearance in the locality. As part of the works the local swimming-pool and laundry facility had been closed. Although the building was not demolished, at the time its future was undecided. Clearly the local ladies, who not only carried out their washing duties there but also saw it as a social gathering place, were not happy about its closure. The ladies who used the laundry would take their washing to Lancaster Road Baths on a regular basis, probably the same day each week, where they would meet the same people and keep up with local gossip – the closure of the baths would mean the end of this institution. The campaign was carried out with passion and the women of the Dale took their fight to Kensington Town Hall. The ladies were a formidable opposition and they eventually got results – they forced the local council into supplying new laundry facilities under the Westway. The new public launderette was not the Lancaster Road Baths, but it was the best they could get.

It wasn't until 1975 that the sad edifice that was Lancaster Road Baths and Wash House was demolished and it was mourned by many. As a school boy at Colville School I learnt to swim there, I gained my swimming certificates there and I knew almost every ceramic tile in both pools – the days of school holidays spent swimming were many and the memories are as vivid as if it was yesterday.

The man-made lake-sized body of standing stagnant water known as the 'Ocean' is another subject that needs further attention, and as an interesting but somewhat sad piece of local history it finds space in this chapter. The area adjacent to the Piggeries was in earlier years known as the Potteries, due to the fact that from the late-eighteenth century bricks and pots had been produced in an area centred on Pottery Lane. Not much remains of this industry now with the exception of a single bottlekiln which stands in a preserved condition at the southern end of Walmer Road. Opposite the kiln is Avondale Park, a peaceful and green area of calm retreat for local people, a safe place for local children to play. The area of the park has not always been so welcoming, and in the heyday of the Potteries and Piggeries the ground that the park now occupies was a notorious lake of putrid water known as the 'Ocean'. The Ocean covered almost an acre of land, which was to give up its yellow London clay as raw materials for the industrious inhabitants of the Potteries, and in return the waste from the pigsties, industrial areas and residential dwellings fed into this open cesspit. In 1848 an outbreak of cholera was to afflict the pitifully poor residents of Notting Dale. Those living in this area succumbed to the illness in such numbers that action had to be taken. The Commissioners of Sewers were forced into supplying standpipes in an effort to make clean water available to the residents, and planned where new sewers would run in an effort to clean up the area of standing water. The work was essential and welcomed, but it was too little too late for many in the Dale – even in 1899 this was an area that was coloured black on the Booth's poverty map, indicating that the area was in the poorest category. The average age expectancy fell to a tragic 11 years seven months and the mortality rate was as high as 50 percent – sad statistics indeed. The 'Ocean' was eventually swept away in 1863 when the clay workings were filled in and the land reclaimed for more social use. Housing improvements were to wait slightly longer with work starting in 1870. We see no trace of what lies beneath Avondale Park – it is a feature of the Dales landscape which, in its passing, was and is mourned by none.

For a long time parts of the Royal Borough of Kensington and Chelsea have been popular with royalty, and indeed even parts of Notting Hill have had a certain amount of royal patronage. However, Notting Dale would not readily spring to mind as an area you could find a king amongst the commoners. It is, of course, not as it may seem when I say 'king',

One of the central figures in the Profumo affair, Mandy Rice-Davies.

because the royal personage that was for a number of years resident amongst the poverty was in fact the so-called King of the Gypsies, a man called Hearn. Hearn was a man described in earlier published works as 'picturesque' and, having no images of him, we must use our imagination as to what was actually meant. As it was known that this man had travelled widely and had fought through the Napoleonic Wars, I personally like to think of him with a dark and furrowed complexion and sharply chiselled features, but what we do know for sure is that this was a man who could drink hard and fight even harder. He was, by nature, a leader and was considered the patriarch of his clan, but at the age of 90, a more than considerable age in the 1860s things were to change for 'old Hearn'.

He had given up his wanderings and settled in the Latimer Road area. This was a time when the missions were working hard to dissuade the locals from their drunkenness. Hearn, for whatever reason, found the mission's efforts to cut the alcoholic pastimes of his people attractive and signed the pledge. The gypsies followed Hearn and turned their backs on travelling, making a more permanent home in the Dale. But that was only the start, in following the example of Hearn they also gave up drunkenness, swearing and even the lucrative business of fortune telling – next to go were the horses. Such was the depth of the change in the gypsies that they even went through marriage services, something that was unheard of in their communities. The transformation was almost complete when the gypsies turned to legitimate employment and applied for hawkers' licences – also, for reasons better known to themselves, they turned their backs on and gave up the Romany language, with the exception of a few words that have survived and can still be heard on the market stalls of Portobello Road. Look carefully and you will still be able to spot the descendants of those gypsy families of 150 years ago – many of the older totters can still be identified by their dark skin and typically market-style outfits, the neckerchief, trilby hat and waistcoat.

One of the most notorious episodes of the 1960s political scene was the scandal that involved a government minister, a pair of call girls and a Russian. The minister was John Profumo and the girls Christine Keeler and Mandy Rice-Davis. Keeler and Rice-Davis were girlfriends of Peter Rachman, and the scandal brought about the downfall of Profumo, and indeed the subsequent fall of the Tory government. The events took place during the height of the Cold War; a government minister sleeping with the same call girl as a senior Russian figure was seen as a possible security risk. It was suspected that the KGB might be involved and it was a scandal from which John Profumo could not recover.

Keeler had been a regular face in 'El Rio's', Frank Crichlow's West Indian café at 127 Westbourne Park Road, and was frequently seen around the Notting Hill area. Crichlow later went on to run another well known café, the Mangrove in All Saints Road. He was a prominent figure in the riots of 1958, and was one of the main protagonists in the Blenheim Crescent battle. The involvement of Rachman's girls in the scandal led to revelations about his business methods coming to light. The incident was the subject of the 1989 film *Scandal* staring Joanne Whalley and John Hurt, as well as the frontman of the pop group, Fine Young Cannibals, Roland Gift and a title song by Dusty Springfield, who incidentally also lived locally for a time. A record was also released by a mysterious artist named Miss X – the song title was 'Christine' and was a satirical effort in 1963 from the pen of John Barry. The mysterious Miss X turned out to be Joyce Blair, wife of actor and dancer Lionel.

Rod Freeman, jazz guitarist, seen here in the early 2000s playing as part a member of a jazz trio.

Andy Sparrows's map of Portobello Road.

Chapter 16

The Art of Notting Hill

The art scene has, for many years, been very active in this part of London. Although I have no idea exactly when it started, I would hazard a guess that it is something that has been here since the early days of the seasonal gypsy camps. Even during the Victorian period there was a thriving artistic base, it may not have been as overt as it is in 2006, but there has always been an undercurrent of the Left Bank feel about the place.

Even by looking around at the blue plaques on many of the buildings we find painters, writers, poets and indeed artists representing almost all disciplines. The problem is very often in deciding what an artist is. Personally, as an engineer, I would nominate Brunel, an odd choice maybe but there is artistry in many of his creations. In my adopted home of the Westcountry is the fabulous structure of the Clifton Suspension Bridge and the newly restored SS *Great Britain,* but back in my real home of West London is a legacy that is as grand as either, and that is the Great West Railway with its awe-inspiring terminus at Paddington. Many will say this is not art and is building or engineering, but because it cannot be hung in the Tate Gallery doesn't mean its merits and beauty should not be admired. It is the case with many of the local artists of today that their recognition may only be local or, if more widely recognised, it tends to be through the medium of the internet, rather than on television or international publications.

My first example of local art and artists is someone who has embraced the twentieth century's most accessible media, the internet, and the form the art takes is of comics. Some may not like this form of art, but it is, in my opinion, a valid and important artform of the twentieth century, indeed evolving from cartoons of much earlier times. There are some fine examples of cartoons that date from the time of the French Revolution and even the more recent examples such as the DC comics of the 1950s are considered to be important and valuable artworks today. Andy Sparrow is a local artist who has lived in the area most of his adult life, and has a fully populated website that is exciting and even a little bit dangerous. I came across his work whilst trawling for research material about Portobello Road and have been popping back for a fix of his 'online comic' ever since. The site includes the interactive map of Portobello Road, a copy of which is shown opposite, but it was also his attitude to art that caught my attention. I quote:

I drew everything on this website for the pleasure of it, not for money. There is no editor to tell me what I can and cannot say; thus because I am free my work (I think) is better. The only person whose reaction is important is you (the reader) and your reaction will be honest because the art is free.

I like Andy Sparrows's work and I am both impressed and inspired by his ethics and attitude.

There is a particularly active rap scene in Notting Hill which may seem fairly obvious, given the fact that it is home to so many West Indian rap artists and also the carnival, which gives them their annual public showcase to exhibit their talents. The rap and performance artist JC001 is a little different, in that he is by no way stereotypical for an artist at the very pinnacle of this form of musical art. JC001 is the son of an Anglo-Irish mother and Anglo-Indian (born in Wales) father. Born in 1966 he was brought up on Ladbroke Grove and honed his art with local artists in and around the area. He was a regular at parties where he performed for the love of it, but his reputation and talent was getting noticed. JC001 signed for Eurythmics's frontman Dave Stewart's 'Anxious' record label in 1988, and also went on to be featured in the *Guinness Book of Records* for being the fastest rapper in 1993. His world record was gained on the BBC Radio 5 show 'The Mix' with an astonishing 631

Not quite graffiti but the painter's art is displayed to good effect on this building in Westbourne Park Road.

Buffy Blakelock singing in the Ladbroke Arms. In the 1960s and '70s pub entertainment was at its peak, and there were always impromptu performances by members of the audience.

The bottom end of St Lukes Mews (originally this section was called Lancaster Mews), with legal graffiti art on the wall of the old Island Records studios.

syllables a minute. Rap may not be everyone's choice but this valid and important form of youth art is a modern incarnation of poetry that has much to say about today's issues. JC001 toured with Shakespear's Sister and in his words 'slipped into the poetry scene'. Readings were in a conventional or a cappella style and resulted in further acknowledgment of his talent. He has been involved in the collaborative work by the English National Opera and the Asian Dub Foundation. JC001 is co-writing and due to perform in a revolutionary opera which is based on the life and influences of Libyan leader Col Muamar Qaddafi, an unusual and controversial subject for an opera, but it is a project that is exciting for JC001 who is also to plays Qaddafi in the production.

Someone that was well known in Notting Hill was Patrick King, a man who had lived for almost 30 years in the area and had built up a reputation as a prolific and particularly talented poet. He could be seen performing in various cafés and venues in the area where, accompanied by a background sound-track of guitar music, his work was almost melodic and even dreamlike. Regrettably, Patrick passed away in 2004, but he will be remembered for his mastery of the spoken and written word.

Looking at a more classical form of art, the Notting Hill area and Ladbroke Square in particular, should be proud that a poet and author of some note counts herself amongst its residents. Ruth Fainlight was born in New York but has lived in the UK since she was 15, with sojourns in both France and Spain. She is married to Alan Sillitoe and spends time at her second home in Somerset. She has had 13 books of poetry and two volumes of short stories published. She received the Cholmondeley Award in 1994 and was shortlisted for the 1998 Whitbread Award for her work *Sugar-Paper Blue*. She is an internationally acclaimed artist who is one of Notting Hill's best-loved residents. From her work *Time and Ladbroke Square* I quote:

But even before the Second World War the district was in decline. First every floor then every room had different tenants. [Today] the houses glisten with new paint and fittings. The rich are back.

Music is, of course, a very important part of the art scene in Notting Hill and it is something that has been briefly touched on in the previous chapters, but it is an artform that is particularly well represented on the street. You cannot walk along Portobello Road without hearing music in one form or another some-where in the street, and you cannot visit many pubs without at some point hearing live music being performed. Amongst the contributors within these pages you will find at least one musician. Rod Freeman is amongst those erstwhile artists who perform within the borough on a regular basis. I asked Rod for a picture of himself performing in the area and which of the pubs and clubs he had indeed

played at – his response was typically Rod: '... it would be easier to say where I haven't played, I think that over the years I have performed in virtually all the venues in and around Notting Hill.' Rod then went on to explain his musical interests. He plays guitar for a three-piece jazz band and performs in many different locations. Again jazz is one of those artforms that is particularly well represented in London W11.

As you would expect from a London borough with a history of markets and market humour, Notting Hill is still a good place to catch up with artists who can and do tell a good gag. The local pubs also have quite a reputation for comedians and comedy in general. The Elgin pub, amongst others, has been up there with many far more famous comedy venues, giving local performers an opportunity to get their acts seen and heard. The artform in the borough goes back a long way – Albert Chevallier was a 'coster comedian' in the 1880s.

Revealed in October 2005, when advertising hoardings were removed from the side wall of the old Co-Op store in All Saints Road, this advertising flyer was for 'Folk at the Oak with Nigel Denver and Friends'. It is believed to be from the 1960s.

Jazz trio 'The Hightown Crows' entertain near the shop used by Hugh Grant in the film Notting Hill.

Notting Hill is the venue for the Portobello Film Festival an event that has grown and is growing into one of the premier events of its type. It showcases films about the area, films by students and professionals and a host of other genres. The event was first put on in 1996, at which time it showed *Performance,* the Nicholas Roeg and Donald Cammel film staring Mick Jagger – a film that has ties with the area – and the John Boorman work *Leo the Last.* A person who was also showcased, and indeed short-listed for the indie section's 'Golden Boot Award', was Guy Ritchie, who was not well known at the time, with his film titled *The Hard Case.* Richie later married Madonna and produced blockbuster films such as *Lock, Stock and Two Smoking Barrels* and *Snatch,* which stared ex-QPR footballer Vinnie Jones. The festival boasts the use of screens in venues as diverse as pubs, marquees and open-air showings. It is an asset to the area and goes to prove, once again, that Notting Hill must have some sort of magic that helps public events become successful.

So the art of Notting Hill is diverse and rich, it ranges from the classical to the ultra modern, it is seen on the streets, in clubs and pubs, it is practiced in schools and in arts centres, but most important of all the art of Notting Hill is of the people, it is a legacy that has and will be seen and felt in this area for a long time.

Chapter 17
The Earl of Shrewsbury and Talbot
The Henry Ford of Notting Hill?

When you think of car production in England the mind naturally turns straight to Dagenham, Longbridge or even Browns Lane, Coventry, but a major player during the early 1900s resided in North Kensington. It is a sad fact that, as with virtually the entire British motor industry, it is no longer in production. The car company we are talking about has been known by several names but in its first incarnation was known as the Clement Talbot Motor Company. The company was set up in 1903 under the patronage of Earl of Shrewsbury and Talbot to import the French Clement car into Britain. The company didn't take long to realise that it could be more profitable by building its own models, and by 1905 it started production of Talbot cars in Barlby Road, and poignantly dropped the Clement part of the name. The venture was not a half-hearted effort and the company saw major success, not only with its road vehicles but also on the race track. Probably its greatest success came in 1913 when Percy Lambert drove a 25-horsepower Talbot in excess of 100 miles within one hour at Brookland race track in Surrey. The car has always been regarded as the first truly 100mph car.

The company was gaining a reputation for building 'well made, fast and efficient cars', and by 1914 had completely ceased to include French components in any of its vehicles. The company had a contract to supply military vehicles to the Russian army, but this was never completely fulfilled – only a few vehicles had been supplied by the beginning of the Russian Revolution, which curtailed any further supply of vehicles.

Over the years military and civil emergency vehicles have been a major part of the company's output, with the supply of vehicles to the Royal Naval Air Service being a contract of particular note. The RNAS had a testing facility at Wormwood Scrubs, which is a mile or so from the Clement Talbot works, and it is believed that the vehicles would have undergone testing there before despatch to various destinations. Stephen Lally of the STD (Sunbeam Talbot Darracq) Register also believes that much of the testing may have been carried out on land adjacent to the Barlby Road plant, and it can be seen from early pictures that the housing estates that are now prevalent in the area were yet to be built at this time. It is also worth noting that the plant itself had a lightly banked test track that ran around the outside of the production buildings. It was clear that a great deal of thought had gone into the design of the track – the buildings were specially shaped to avoid sharp corners and provide easier entry for the cars into the bends.

The company went from strength to strength up until the start of the First World War, when the plant was turned over to the production of ambulances. Unfortunately Talbot never really recovered from this break in civil production and was taken over by Darracq, a Paris-based but British-controlled company in 1919. The newly formed Talbot Darracq Company didn't fair too well and it became a prime target for an amalgamation, which happened in 1925 when Sunbeam joined Talbot Darracq to form STD.

The new company was good for Talbot and its fortunes started to turn, mainly due to a huge amount of support from the much more successful Sunbeam arm of the company.

By the late 1920s Talbot employed a Swiss chief engineer named Georges Roesch, who designed new and more exciting engines for Talbot. This new era in the company's history was the best thing for Talbot

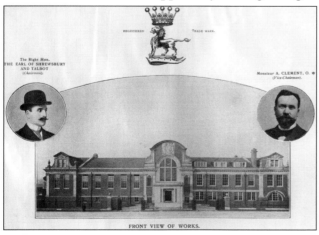

From an early publication (mid-1900s) from the Clement Talbot Company showing the faces of the Earl of Shrewsbury and Talbot, Chairman and Monsieur Adolph Clement, Vice Chairman and the front of the Clement Talbot works in Barlby Road.

The Barlby Road works of Clement Talbot in 1903. The façade of Ladbroke Hall remains as it did when it was built, but the factory buildings have all gone and been replaced with a housing estate.

The entrance of Ladbroke Hall, complete with an impressive display of silverware and trophies, early 1900s.

The Clement Talbot engine room. Note the impressive plaque on the wall – a somewhat extravagant piece for an engine room.

The chassis workshop in 1905.

Final assembly of the motor vehicles.

The machine shop with its shaft and belt-drive system for powering the machines, 1905.

Film star Gladys Cooper with her 10/23 Talbot in 1923.

Talbot's private test track running around the outside of the workshop complex.

Military personnel outside the Barlby Road works during the First World War.

Kitty Brunel was a well-known rally driver of the 1920s and '30s. Clearly she also knew what went on under the bonnet of her 1929 14/45 Talbot motorcar.

The engine assembly shop. A full refurbishment of the factory took place in the 1930s. Note the lack of shaft and belt drives.

A Talbot-built ambulance in the livery of Kent County Council, 1930s.

Two particularly impressive examples of the Talbot marques outside Ladbroke Hall, 1930s.

HRH The Prince of Wales on a tour of the factory in the 1930s.

The finished product outside the front of Ladbroke Hall. This is a ten-horsepower model, the first built under the Rootes banner. It was actually a re-bodied Hillman Minx.

An early Talbot advert.

and it became the dominant element of the STD group of companies.

In the period between 1922 and 1927 Sunbeam had been amongst the premier manufacturers in motorsport and had won grand prix and land-speed records with Kenelm Lee Guinness at Brooklands and Major Henry Segrave at Southport, and also supplied engines for Sir Malcolm Campbell's Pendine Sands attempt in 'Bluebird', which is probably the most famous land-speed record. Sunbeam's last successful attempt on the world record came in 1927 at Daytona when Segrave achieved a speed of 203.79mph. He utilised twin V12 engines, giving a total output in excess of 1,000 horsepower.

The Sunbeam name was synonymous with motor racing in the 1920s, and if you were to ask a schoolboy during that period what car he dreamed of owning he would undoubtedly reply 'Sunbeam' – mentioning the name these days would no doubt draw a blank look.

The fortunes of the STD Company finally waned in 1934 and it went into receivership before being broken up. The Rootes Group bought the still-successful Talbot part of the company in 1935 but rapidly phased out the Talbot models in favour of re-badged Hillman and Humber vehicles. They also managed to steal the Sunbeam marque from under the nose of Henry Lyons's SS (Swallow Sidecars) company, a company that has outlived both Talbot and Sunbeam since changing names after the war from SS to the immensely successful Jaguar cars.

The war years were to be another phase in the life of Sunbeam Talbot during which production of civilian vehicles ceased. However, its wartime record is unrivalled. The company produced the Hillman Minx and Humber Snipes for military use, but the major part of its production went into the development of bombers, bombs and armoured vehicles. The figures are astonishing and through the war Rootes was responsible for producing 14 per cent of the RAF's requirement for bombers, and also manufactured 60 per cent of the country's armoured cars, 35 per cent of its scout cars, 50,000 aero engines and 300,000 bombs. This level of production required a new factory, as a result of which Rootes were given new premises at Ryton, and William Rootes was given a knighthood.

There is a report by Megan Davies, an employee of Sunbeam Talbot, that:

Following a particularly heavy air raid, I came into the Barlby Road plant to find a piece of a headstone from Kensal Green Cemetery on my desk which had been blown through the skylight, the cemetery is at least a half a mile away. The inscription read 'rest in peace'.

When normal production recommenced in 1945 only two models were being produced and, with the new plant at Ryton working below full volume, the fate of the Barlby Road site was inevitable. In 1946 all production in London ceased and was transferred to the new Ryton facility, and only repair and service work was carried out at Barlby Road.

In later years the factory became a studio for Thames Television Company, but in 2006 has mostly been demolished and replaced with a housing estate, although the old façade and a few bits of the old Rootes Hall remain.

The logo of the Sunbeam Talbot Darracq Register.

Chapter 18

Further Revelations

I had stopped adding chapters when things in London got a little worrying. On Thursday 7 July 2005, 56 people died as a result of suicide bombers on three underground trains and a bus. Whilst I have no wish to politicise this book the events of that day and what was to follow were eventually to have an indelible impact on Notting Hill.

The following Thursday would see me making my way from my home up into Notting Hill to continue my research into this book. It was a hot, sunny summer's day, unlike the previous Thursday which had started wet and dull and just continued to get worse as the terrorists carried out their atrocities in our fabulous city. London was to mourn its dead with a three-minute silence on Thursday 14 July, the day I had chosen to once again visit Notting Hill. This sign of respect was marked all over London and indeed in many other cities throughout the world. It was a poignant and sobering occasion but one that Londoners wanted to mark and was what they needed in order to show their grief and unity. My day continued as planned with productive meetings with various contributors and I left North Kensington at around 5.30pm to make my way home.

The following Thursday, July 21, was again to be a day that would make the headlines. Once again suicide bombers would try to ply their deadly trade in London and, indeed, this time in our part of the capital. Four terrorists attempted – unsuccessfully – to detonate bombs on the underground and a bus. Whether by luck, divine intervention or some other unseen hand all four devices failed to detonate. One of these terrorists had joined the London underground network at Westbourne Park Station heading on to Shepherd's Bush, where he tried to detonate his device. This was the first part of the community to be touched by this series of incidents but it was not the last.

Another chapter in the story takes us to the park land at the end of North Pole Road, Little Wormwood Scrubs, a small piece of grass-covered land that was once earmarked to be a local cemetery. A fifth member of the Al Qaeda suicide cell probably gave up his mission when his bomb also failed to detonate fully. He later dumped his device in a bush on this small piece of green.

With all four or possibly five bombers at large the security forces now concentrated their efforts on locating them. The first would be caught in Birmingham but Friday July 29 would be another day to go down in the history of North Kensington. Bombers two and three were caught in the Peabody estate, just a stone's throw from Little Wormwood Scrubs, whilst number four, the so-called Shepherd's Bush bomber would be caught in Rome. Tavistock Crescent would also become an integral part of the story, with the arrest of a fifth suspect, believed to be the person who disposed of his bomb on Little Wormwood Scrubs. This chapter in our district's history was being played out on primetime TV, news programmes updating from the streets of Notting Hill on a minute-by-minute basis, and all the time the long-suffering residents accepting whatever was happening on their streets. Again I am proud of the people of London and proud to be a Londoner and must repeat a message that was seen and heard in London over these difficult few weeks, 'We will not be beaten'.

This particular attack on London and its subsequent impact on Notting Hill is not the first time that the area has had to deal with terrorism. During the height of the troubles in Northern Ireland a bomb was set off killing one person in the Holland Park area. A few years later in 1981 an attack by Neo Nazis on the carnival was foiled by special branch officers. A group of extremists with links to European groups that had carried out an attack on the Munich beer festival had planned carnage at the Notting Hill carnival. The plan was to send a suitcase bomber into a crowded part of the carnival and detonate the bomb. The carrier, not expecting the bomb to detonate at that time, would also have been killed. This was a ploy used by the European groups to avoid leaving a suspect that could break under interrogation. Following what would have been carnage, snipers in adjacent windows would open fire on the police and emergency services in an effort to provoke confrontation between the Afro-Caribbean community and the security forces. Fortunately these events were thwarted before anyone was killed or even hurt and race relations were left on a solid footing.

We all – Londoners, visitors and anyone that believes in peace – must hope and pray that those with the intent to destroy our way of life and the peace of our city fail. The community we have in Notting Hill is a fine example of how different races, creeds and religions can and should live together in peace.

Appendix
Notting Hill in Pictures, 2006

Above: *Freshly prepared seafood while you wait.*

Left: *Sara Sanskara. Sara sells particularly colourful and flamboyant designs from her pitch in Portobello Road.*

'The Hightown Crows' start to gather an audience. Behind is the back entrance to Colville Junior School.

Even in March some brave the cold to sit on the roof terrace overlooking the hustle and bustle of a busy Saturday on Portobello Road.

A slice of pizza and a gate to lean on. These two young ladies enjoy the spring sunshine and a bite to eat.

Above: *Morning coffee, and a chance to chat and browse the handbags on display.*

Inset, top right: *Even on market days the mail must be delivered. Eddie the postman on his round in Portobello Road.*

A place to meet, relax and watch the world go by.

Refills for wallets hold up traffic in Notting Hill. The queue is for the cash machine (ATM) at the bank on the corner of Colville Terrace.

'Do you really think we will all fit in there?'

An antiques dealer in Portobello Road.

A view from the business side of a stall in Portobello Road. Musical instruments, pocket watches, jewellery and even a cuddly toy – the traders in Portobello Road can sell anything.

Necklaces and pendants by the hundred – many are handmade by the artisans that run the stalls.

Pam with her world-famous and award-winning button stall at Portobello Green. A picture of the Beatles looks on from the window of the adjacent tailor's shop.

Right: *Carl is a familiar face around Portobello Green.*

Below: *Pam, Chuck and Errol are members of the Portobello Green community.*

It may look like junk but it is amazing what people will buy. This pitch in Golborne is particularly well stocked.

A fine display of second-hand shoes and jackets.

THE BOOK OF NOTTING HILL

Subscribers

June and Eddie Adams, Notting Hill, London

Malcolm Ashman, Harefield

Martin Botwright, Notting Hill, London

Nellie Brazier, Reading, Berkshire

James Buckley, Lansdowne Road

Roger and Dave Catt

Hanna Conway, Bayswater

Robert Cook, Notting Dale

Damian Donnelly, Lancaster West EMB

John Earley, Lonsdale Road. 1948–1971

Jason G. Evans, Warminster, Wiltshire

Adele and Markus Fiala, Portobello Road, Notting Hill

The Griffin Family, Notting Hill, London

Mr Luke Kirton, Brentford

Benjamin Lamberg, Notting Hill

Rosina Layton, Melbourne, Australia

Ron and Sharon Macmillan, Warminster, Wiltshire

Maureen Marshall, Ruislip

Mr Charles William Morgan, Bexhill on Sea, East Sussex

Notting Hill Preparatory School

Mrs M. Porter, Elgin Crescent, Notting Hill

Jackie and Tony Rawlings, Truro, Cornwall

Jean Saunders (née Block)

Mrs M.G. Summers

James J.R. Terry, Notting Hill, London

Thomas Jones Primary School

Mr Robin Tuck, Notting Hill, W10

John F.W. Walling, Newton Abbot, Devon

Linda and Ray Wilkinson, Ealing

Mrs Jennifer Williams, Llantwit Fardre, Wales

Mr A.S. Woodford, Wesley Square, Notting Barn

Community Histories: Further Reading

The Book of Addiscombe • Canning and Clyde Road Residents Association and Friends
The Book of Addiscombe, Vol. II • Canning and Clyde Road Residents Association and Friends
The Book of Ashburton • Stuart Hands and Pete Webb
The Book of Axminster with Kilmington • Les Berry and Gerald Gosling
* *The Book of Axmouth & the Undercliff* • Ted Gosling and Mike Clement
The Book of Bakewell • Trevor Brighton
The Book of Bampton • Caroline Seward
The Book of Barnstaple • Avril Stone
The Book of Barnstaple, Vol. II • Avril Stone
The Book of The Bedwyns • Bedwyn History Society
* *The Book of Bere Regis* • Rodney Legg and John Pitfield
The Book of Bergh Apton • Geoffrey I. Kelly
The Book of Bickington • Stuart Hands
The Book of Bideford • Peter Christie and Alison Grant
Blandford Forum: A Millennium Portrait • Blandford Forum Town Council
* *The Book of Blofield* • Barbara Pilch
The Book of Boscastle • Rod and Anne Knight
The Book of Bourton-on-the-Hill, Batsford and Sezincote • Allen Firth
The Book of Bramford • Bramford Local History Group
The Book of Breage & Germoe • Stephen Polglase
The Book of Bridestowe • D. Richard Cann
* *The Book of Bridgwater* • Roger Evans
The Book of Bridport • Rodney Legg
The Book of Brixham • Frank Pearce
The Book of Buckfastleigh • Sandra Coleman
The Book of Buckland Monachorum & Yelverton • Pauline Hamilton-Leggett
The Book of Budleigh Salterton • D. Richard Cann
The Book of Carharrack • Carharrack Old Cornwall Society
The Book of Carshalton • Stella Wilks and Gordon Rookledge
The Parish Book of Cerne Abbas • Vivian and Patricia Vale

The Book of Chagford • Iain Rice
The Book of Chapel-en-le-Frith • Mike Smith
The Book of Chittlehamholt with Warkleigh & Satterleigh • Richard Lethbridge
The Book of Chittlehampton • Various
The Book of Codford • Romy Wyeth
The Book of Colney Heath • Bryan Lilley
The Book of Constantine • Moore and Trethowan
The Book of Cornwood and Lutton • Compiled by the People of the Parish
The Book of Crediton • John Heal
The Book of Creech St Michael • June Small
The Book of Crowcombe, Bicknoller and Sampford Brett • Maurice and Joyce Chidgey
The Book of Crudwell • Tony Pain
The Book of Cullompton • Compiled by the People of the Parish
The Book of Dawlish • Frank Pearce
The Book of Dulverton, Brushford, Bury & Exebridge • Dulverton and District Civic Society
The Book of Dunster • Hilary Binding
The Book of Easton • Easton Village History Project
The Book of Edale • Gordon Miller
The Ellacombe Book • Sydney R. Langmead
* *The Book of Elmsett* • Elmsett Local History Group
The Book of Exmouth • W.H. Pascoe
* *The Book of Fareham* • Lesley Burton and Brian Musselwhite
The Book of Grampound with Creed • Bane and Oliver
The Book of Gosport • Lesley Burton and Brian Musselwhite
The Book of Haughley • Howard Stephens
The Book of Hayle • Harry Pascoe
The Book of Hayling Island & Langstone • Peter Rogers
The Book of Helston • Jenkin with Carter
The Book of Hemyock • Clist and Dracott
The Book of Herne Hill • Patricia Jenkyns
The Book of Hethersett • Hethersett Society Research Group
The Book of High Bickington • Avril Stone

The Book of Honiton • Gerald Gosling
The Book of Ilsington • Dick Wills
* *The Book of Kessingland* • Maureen and
Eric Long
The Book of Kingskerswell • Carsewella Local
History Group
The Book of Lamerton • Ann Cole and Friends
Lanner, A Cornish Mining Parish • Sharron
Schwartz and Roger Parker
The Book of Leigh & Bransford • Malcolm Scott
The Second Book of Leigh & Bransford •
Malcolm Scott
The Book of Litcham with Lexham & Mileham •
Litcham Historical and Amenity Society
The Book of Loddiswell • Loddiswell Parish
History Group
The New Book of Lostwithiel • Barbara Fraser
The Book of Lulworth • Rodney Legg
The Book of Lustleigh • Joe Crowdy
The Book of Lydford • Compiled by
Barbara Weeks
The Book of Lyme Regis • Rodney Legg
The Book of Manaton • Compiled by the
Peopleof the Parish
The Book of Markyate • Markyate Local
History Society
The Book of Mawnan • Mawnan Local
History Group
The Book of Meavy • Pauline Hemery
The Book of Mere • Dr David Longbourne
The Book of Minehead with Alcombe • Binding
and Stevens
The Book of Monks Orchard and Eden Park •
Ian Muir and Pat Manning
The Book of Morchard Bishop • Jeff Kingaby
* *Mount Batten – The Flying Boats of Plymouth* •
Gerald Wasley
* *The Book of Mulbarton* • Jill and
David Wright
The Book of Mylor • Mylor Local History Group
The Book of Narborough • Narborough Local
History Society
The Book of Newdigate • John Callcut
The Book of Newtown • Keir Foss
The Book of Nidderdale • Nidderdale
Museum Society
The Book of Northlew with Ashbury • Northlew
History Group
The Book of North Newton • J.C. and K.C. Robins
The Book of North Tawton • Baker, Hoare
and Shields
* *The Book of Notting Hill* • Melvin Wilkinson

The Book of Nynehead • Nynehead & District
History Society
The Book of Okehampton • Roy and
Ursula Radford
The Book of Ottery St Mary • Gerald Gosling
and Peter Harris
The Book of Paignton • Frank Pearce
The Book of Penge, Anerley & Crystal Palace •
Peter Abbott
The Book of Peter Tavy with Cudlipptown •
Peter Tavy Heritage Group
The Book of Pimperne • Jean Coull
The Book of Plymtree • Tony Eames
The Book of Poole • Rodney Legg
* *The Book of Porchfield & Locks Green* • Keir Foss
The Book of Porlock • Dennis Corner
* *The Book of Portland* • Rodney Legg
Postbridge – The Heart of Dartmoor • Reg Bellamy
The Book of Priddy • Albert Thompson
The Book of Princetown • Dr Gardner-Thorpe
The Book of Probus • Alan Kent and
Danny Merrifield
The Book of Rattery • By the People of
the Parish
The Book of Roadwater, Leighland and Treborough
• Clare and Glyn Court
* *The Book of St Audries and West Quantoxhead* •
Duncan Stafford
The Book of St Austell • Peter Hancock
The Book of St Day • Joseph Mills and
Paul Annear
The Book of St Dennis and Goss Moor •
Kenneth Rickard
* *The Book of St Ervan* • Moira Tangye
The Book of St Levan • St Levan Local
History Group
The Book of Sampford Courtenay
with Honeychurch • Stephanie Pouya
The Book of Sculthorpe • Gary Windeler
The Book of Seaton • Ted Gosling
The Book of Sidmouth • Ted Gosling and
Sheila Luxton
The Book of Silverton • Silverton Local
History Society
The Book of South Molton • Jonathan Edmunds
The Book of South Stoke with Midford • Edited
by Robert Parfitt
South Tawton & South Zeal with Sticklepath • Roy
and Ursula Radford
*The Book of Sparkwell with Hemerdon &
Lee Mill* • Pam James
* *The Book of Spetisbury* • Ann Taylor

The Book of Staverton • Pete Lavis
The Book of Stithians • Stithians Parish
History Group
*The Book of Stogumber, Monksilver, Nettlecombe
& Elworthy* • Maurice and Joyce Chidgey
The Book of South Brent • Greg Wall
The Book of Studland • Rodney Legg
The Book of Swanage • Rodney Legg
The Book of Tavistock • Gerry Woodcock
* *The Book of Thatcham* • Peter Allen
The Book of Thorley • Sylvia McDonald and Bill
Hardy
The Book of Torbay • Frank Pearce
The Book of Truro • Christine Parnell
The Book of Uplyme • Gerald Gosling and Jack
Thomas
The Book of Watchet • Compiled by David Banks
*The Book of Wendling, Longham and Beeston with
Bittering* • Stephen Olley
The Book of West Huntspill • By the People
of the Parish
The Book of Weston-super-Mare • Sharon Poole
* *The Book of Whippingham* • Sarah Burdett
The Book of Whitchurch • Gerry Woodcock
Widecombe-in-the-Moor • Stephen Woods
Widecombe – Uncle Tom Cobley & All •
Stephen Woods
The Book of Williton • Michael Williams
* *The Book of Wilton* • Chris Rousell
The Book of Wincanton • Rodney Legg
The Book of Winscombe • Margaret Tucker
The Book of Witheridge • Peter and Freda Tout
and John Usmar
The Book of Withycombe • Chris Boyles
Woodbury: The Twentieth Century Revisited •
Roger Stokes
The Book of Woolmer Green • Compiled by the
People of the Parish
The Book of Yetminster • Shelagh Hill
* *The Book of Veryan & Portloe* • Diana Smith and
Christine Parnell

For details of any of the above titles or if you
are interested in writing your own history,
please contact: Commissioning Editor,
Community Histories, Halsgrove House,
Lower Moor Way, Tiverton, Devon EX16 6SS,
England; email: katyc@halsgrove.com

* 2006 publications